flavored oils

Noreen-
I hope you enjoy this
infusion of recipes.
Keep Cooking.

Michael Churchill

To my wife, Ines,
and my mother, Antoniette, the two greatest inspirations in my life.

ACKNOWLEDGMENTS

This book is a product of my never-ending pursuit of great tasting food.
That search has brought me in contact with many people
who have participated in the creation of this book, both directly and indirectly.

To the staff of Tra Vigne restaurant and the Cantinetta for their patience
during my alchemist periods
and especially for their support of my dreams.

To my partners, Bill Upson, Bill Higgins, Kevin Cronin, and
Cindy Pawlcyn for providing me with room
to breathe and to grow and a stage on which to perform.

To Dr. Moshé Shifrine for his technical collaboration, creative
encouragement, and shelf stability!

To all the management and staff of Napa Valley Kitchens for believing
great food can also be simple.

To Maria Syms for her organization and calm skill in helping me
test all the recipes for this book and to all the
friends who came on Monday nights to eat and critique.
They made writing the book fun and gave it a sense of purpose:
that good food brings good friends together.

To Darrell Corti for his friendship and support and for generously
sharing his research on California olive oil.

To Penni Wisner, scribe, friend, and coach. For
her understanding of the life of a chef and for, more often than not,
knowing what I am trying to say better than I do.
This journal of recipes would
not have been possible without her guiding hand and hard work.

Flavored Oils

50 Recipes for Cooking with Infused Oils

by Michael Chiarello with Penelope Wisner

Photography by Daniel Proctor

CHRONICLE BOOKS

SAN FRANCISCO

Library of Congress Cataloging-in-Publication Data:

Chiarello, Michael.
    Flavored oils: 50 recipes for cooking with infused oils/by
  Michael Chiarello with Penelope Wisner; photography by Daniel Proctor.
       p.   cm.
    Includes index.
    ISBN 0-8118-0898-X
    1. Cookery (Olive oil) 2. Spices. I. Wisner, Penelope. II. Title.
  TX819.042C45 1995
  641.6′ 463—dc20   94-27961
                                                 CIP

Food stylist: M. Susan Broussard
Printed in Hong Kong.

Distributed in Canada
by Raincoast Books
8680 Cambie Street
Vancouver, B.C. V6P 6M9

10 9 8 7 6 5 4 3 2 1

Chronicle Books
275 Fifth Street
San Francisco, CA 94103

CONTENTS

Whenever my *nonna* (grandmother) made tomato sauce from her own canned tomatoes, she would send my mother to the basement for a spoonful of *conserva*, a mixture of puréed dried tomatoes and olive oil. The intensity of flavor added a mouthful of summer to her wintertime sauce. She also used the flavorful oil that floated to the top of the *conserva* to drizzle over vegetables roasted atop her wood-fired stove. This tradition was passed on to me by my mother.

This aromatic *conserva* was my first exposure to infused oils. It was a product, a by-product really, of a way of life: At the end of summer my family began preserving the harvest to eat through the winter. We dried the tomatoes on big sheets outdoors. When they were three-quarters dried, they were puréed with olive oil, put in a large crock, and carried to the basement. The lid was another layer of olive oil. As the *conserva* sat, the oil would naturally separate out and float to the top. The oil's passage through the sun-ripened and dried tomatoes gave the *conserva* all the flavor of the summer garden.

My family emigrated from Calabria in southern Italy to the mountains of northern California. They were trades-people: carpenters on my father's side and agricultural people on my mother's side — herdsmen, cheese makers, butchers— following the patterns they had followed for generations in Italy. They learned these trades as part of the natural rhythm of nature: You owned a cow to feed the family and that made you a herdsman, a cheese maker when there was extra milk, and eventually a butcher.

In my mother's kitchen, I learned that Italian cuisine is essentially a cuisine of preservation: Meats became pancetta and prosciutto, milk turned into cheeses, grapes became wine, olives were harvested and brined or cured for eating and pressed for oil. The oil in turn was used to preserve foods as diverse as wild mushrooms we collected in the woods or the garden's tomatoes. The quality of our family meals depended entirely on the quality of our harvest.

The ingredients available to you and their quality will define your cooking style. They do mine. Because I believe this so strongly, as soon as I came to the Napa Valley in 1986 to take charge of the kitchen at the new Tra Vigne restaurant, I focused on our ingredients. We cured our own olives, found our own source of olive oil, and now have our own press. We baked bread, cured meats, made cheeses. These basic ingredients allowed us to build a unique, identifiable regional style of cooking.

The pace of life today and the desire for lighter-tasting foods continue to change the way we cook and eat. In restaurants the days of multicourse meals and complicated dishes are gone. Even at home a one-pot supper must be complete in itself — blending colors, aromas, tastes, and textures. Such simple cooking requires impeccable ingredients — seasonal produce combined with the best of regional products — flavors that stand up and speak for themselves.

As I continued to develop ingredients with big, bold flavors for the restaurant, I started making herb "slurries." These were simple purées made from masses of fresh herbs and olive oil. They added concentrated flavor, color, and a new texture to dishes. I discovered that filtering out the solids kept the oils' taste fresher longer. Soon we were making flavored oils regularly for use in our restaurant kitchen as well as for sale in our little shop, the Cantinetta, in Tra Vigne's courtyard.

Making infused oils will harness the flavor of an ingredient and often makes it easier to cook with. For instance, I love the taste of lavender and use a lavender-infused oil in several dishes, including a roast salmon (page 87). Classic, simple dishes such as a mozzarella, basil, and tomato salad draw new inspiration with flavored oils. At Tra Vigne we present the salad as three cubes of fresh cheese strung on a skewer, topped with roasted peppers and a chiffonade of basil. The cheese sits in a green pool of basil oil flecked with a reduction of balsamic vinegar. When tomatoes are in season, they replace the peppers.

Flavored oils, which can capture and preserve the aroma and flavor of an herb at the peak of its season, add depth and strength to kitchen pantries and shorten cooking times. They work in the kitchen as a condiment —to drizzle on top of foods such as pasta, bruschettas, vegetables, and fish and to stir into sauces and soups. They also work as an ingredient—as a substitute for the fresh ingredient when it has gone out of season, perhaps, or if you have not had time to go to the store. In addition, because flavored oils are olive oil, they are versatile and easy to use—as much at home for sautéing as for making vinaigrettes and sauces.

Flavored olive oils are so incredibly versatile, you might soon find yourself using them in nearly every dish you cook. In a small book, I can only introduce you to a few ideas and recipes. Hopefully, these will encourage you to experiment and explore further.

I have included several techniques for making flavored oils at home. One is used for soft-leaved green herbs such as basil, chervil, and mint; another for more resinous herbs such as lavender, rosemary, and oregano, plus separate methods for roasted garlic and citrus flavored oils.

There are an increasing number of good flavored oils on the market. Flavored oils will vary in flavor depending on the production process, as well as the quality and the specific blend of their ingredients. Taste them before you use them!

The popularity of our homemade flavored oils at Tra Vigne encouraged us to begin commercial production, developing first a basil oil for our Consorzio™ brand in 1992. This initial foray proved so successful that Consorzio now produces roasted garlic, porcini, rosemary, oregano, and five-pepper flavored olive oils. We also produce a garlic, jalapeño, cilantro, and mustard spiced oil for our Napa Valley Kitchens label.

The recipes in this book are grouped into chapters based on flavor—for instance, basil oil or rosemary oil. Each chapter contains a medley of recipes including salads, pasta, fish, meat, and vegetable dishes, as well as a few basic sauces and marinades. They are quickly prepared and simply cooked. You will need very little equipment—a big pot for cooking pasta and blanching vegetables, deep sauté pans, and a few baking dishes. Many of the recipes are modern adaptations of family recipes I learned from my mother. They are meant for everyday eating and enjoyment. All the recipes also may be very successfully cooked *without* flavored olive oils! Use virgin or extra-virgin olive oil and fresh herbs!

Before you start cooking, I would like to give you a few very simple, basic rules. They may contradict some of what you have been taught but, if you follow them, I guarantee you will become a better cook!

- ☺ *Don't cook if you don't want to.*
- ☺ *Don't cook when you are full.*
- ☺ *Shop when you are hungry.*
- ☺ *Cook with those ingredients in the biggest displays. This is usually produce at the peak of its season.*
- ☺ *Make the food your own — substitute and experiment — just never say "I can't make it because I don't have that exact ingredient."*

"Plant grapes for your children and olives for your grandchildren"-Italian proverb

No ingredient plays a more important role in an Italian kitchen than olive oil. When I arrived in the Napa Valley in 1986 to take over the kitchen at Tra Vigne, I needed to find an olive oil to match my style of cooking. My traditional Italian upbringing (in central California but still very Old World) made me want to make one of my own. It had to be a dual-purpose oil, good for cooking and as a condiment.

I began working with various producers of California olive oil and in 1988 bottled our first extra-virgin oil for our Olio Santo label. It was and is still a blend of Mission and Manzanillo olives. The oil tastes fruity, full bodied, and rich and takes the heat well, maintaining its flavor. With this introduction to California olive oil, I became curious about the old olive groves I noticed scattered throughout the Napa Valley and wondered how an olive oil made from the fruit of those trees would taste.

I discovered some of the groves, lost in tangles of brush, oaks, and manzanita while mushroom hunting in the hills surrounding Napa Valley. They did not look like any olive varieties I had seen before. Learning what sort of oil those trees could produce would mean harvesting and pressing the olives in separate small batches, grove by grove. At that time, I could find no one with the capacity to process such small amounts of olives. On a trip to Italy, I found a small, one-half-ton mill and press and brought

it back to the Napa Valley. In 1991 I began pressing olives from these old groves and those of neighbors.

These old trees stand witness that California has a long olive-growing history. Olives arrived in California after 1769 with the Spanish-born Franciscan missionaries. They planted the land surrounding their missions with the essentials of their religious practice and diet: most notably grapes, olives, and wheat. The already established missions in Baja California probably supplied the planting stock for the new California missions, which spread from San Diego to Sonoma, just west of the Napa Valley.

To plant olives, one must have a long-term commitment: The olive trees the padres tended would not bear fully until they were about five years old and would not be considered mature until they were thirty. They would outlive the original Franciscans by decades and continue to produce until they were well over a century in age. Mission olives, brought by the Franciscans and named after the missions where they were first introduced in California, are still the most widely planted variety.

In the 1870s and 1880s California's olive oil industry profited from the importation of many other European olive varieties. New groves were established and press houses sprung up all over the state, including small ones in Napa Valley. Many of the press houses were owned by large olive grove proprietors who sold cured olives in bulk as well. There was not yet an olive canning industry.

Since then, the state's olive oil business has ridden a boom and bust roller coaster. Good olive oil is expensive because of the hand labor required by production, the slowness of the trees to produce, and their inconsistent crop bearing. These qualities help make cultivating olives for olive oil production a business vulnerable to competition.

The invention of the canned ripe olive at the turn of the century sounded the death knell of California's olive oil industry. Canned olives are more profitable than olive oil. In addition, before World War I, cheap, imported olive oil flooded the market. These oils were adulterated with cheaper oils of other types. Eventually, such adulterations of oils and other food products would lead to the Pure Food and Drug Act. California producers fought the imports by telling customers to buy California oil to ensure they were purchasing "pure," unadulterated olive oil. This is perhaps the origin of the now outdated label terminology: pure olive oil.

Our producers enjoyed a respite from cheap competition during the First World War when most of the olive oil producing countries of Europe were at war. At the close of the war, cheap imports again became available until World War II when the pattern repeated itself. During this upheaval many groves were abandoned and forgotten as underbrush grew up around the old trees. Other groves were grafted to canning varieties which have small pits and more flesh than olives for olive oil.

In the last ten years we have experienced an abrupt change. Quite suddenly, there is a resurgent interest in olive oil and its potential quality in California. My own experiments reflect a broader trend. The attitude and excitement is reminiscent of our wine industry when we began to understand we could produce wines equal to the best in the world. As it is, California now grows 99 percent of all olives produced in the United States.

The motivating factor, as it was in the wine industry, has been an educated, demanding consumer. In an enthusiastic heat to get started, the new and hopeful olive oil producers have done everything at once: hired consultants, unearthed and imported traditional equipment including milling stones, set up press houses, harvested from trees thought only decorative a few years ago, imported olive varieties from France and Italy to plant, and bottled single "estate" olive oils.

Because of the high cost of land, equipment, and labor, California will most likely remain a very small producer of olive oil by world standards. My hope is that we will continue to experiment and refine our techniques in order to create oils that are truly expressive of the land and the people, and thus ideally suited to the local cuisine.

CALIFORNIA OLIVE OIL PRODUCTION

In many parts of the world, it is not unusual for a property (anything from a small farm to a large estate) to produce much of the food eaten at its table. Wine, bread, fruit, vegetables, olive oil, meat —all could be grown, harvested, and processed on the same land. Because the soil, the climate, and the people are different on each property, the products it produces develop unique flavors. My dream is to incorporate some of this philosophy into the lifestyle of the inhabitants of Napa Valley.

Olives and olive oil are never the same year to year. Weather conditions vary and the quality and crop level of the olive tree will display these variations. Olive trees of the same type—and there are hundreds of varieties grown for olive oil production— growing a short distance apart in the Napa Valley will produce olive oils that reflect in their taste the very specific conditions surrounding them: the amount of sunlight and water as well as the amount and type of nutrients in the soil. Each variety of olive adds its nuance of character, as do the grower's decisions that affect each tree, most importantly pruning technique and the timing of harvest.

The old groves I work with now to produce individual bottlings had not been pruned in many years. These trees have grown tall; olives are usually pruned into a short, spreading shape to ease hand harvesting and to encourage crop yield. Olive trees bear only on that year's growth; so the crop an unpruned tree bears is sparse and the olives are small. Restoring a grove to production takes time and involves some risk. Over time, as the trees are properly cared for, the crop will change to produce more and fatter olives, hopefully. Only after ten years or so of cultivation and production will I know whether their oil has been worth the effort. For instance, some groves were planted as rootstock, not as fruit-bearing trees. These may never produce good olive oil, and they are too old to graft.

Olives picked early in the season, while they are still green, tend to produce oils with a deep green color and peppery flavors particularly well suited for beans, vegetables, game, and meat. Those picked later in the season, when the olives have begun to change color — from green to a reddish purple — often have a straw-like color and soft, fruity flavors with a vanilla quality good for use with fish.

Production processes are relatively simple and require lots of hard work. Pickers of early harvest olives tape their fingers and strap a basket to their chests. They rake the olives with their fingers off the limbs into the baskets. It is very hard work — green olives cling hard to the tree.

Later in the season, the olives hang more loosely from the tree. In Europe, nets are spread on the ground or suspended under each tree and the limbs are beaten and raked with long poles. There are also mechanical harvesters that grab each tree by the trunk and shake it vigorously. In California, almost all olives are picked green and therefore must be harvested by hand. Now, growers are experimenting with various planting and training systems to allow mechanical harvesting. A full 60 percent of the cost of producing olive oil pays for picking labor alone. Cost-effective harvesting is the biggest stumbling block to building a larger olive oil industry.

Olives must not be bruised or otherwise damaged during picking or processing. Just as a bruise on a peach or pear can lead to rot within a short time, in olives, damage begins a process of oxidation that raises the acidity level. The riper, black olives naturally have higher acidity than green and also are more easily bruised. Picking late-harvest olives in order to make virgin olive oil (which must have a low natural acidity) becomes a high wire act.

After picking, the olives are crushed to a paste. The paste is then mixed which allows the tiny droplets of oil within the cell structure of the olive to adhere to each other and form drops which may then be separated from the olive pits and residue. There are several methods of crushing and mixing, the most picturesque and traditional of which is the massive, stone mill. Two huge, rotating stones crush the olives very slowly between them. The movement of the stones and their slowness allows mixing to take place at the same time. Olives may also be crushed by a hammer mill. Its many small heads shaped like hammers quickly crush the olives by beating them into a paste. The paste must then be mixed well to allow the small droplets of oil to adhere to each other; when well mixed, the paste has a shiny, oily look.

Now the liquid contents of the olives (oil and water) must be separated from the solids, and then the water separated from the oil. In the traditional method, the olive paste is spread on round mats that are stacked in a mechanical hydraulic press. As pressure is applied, the oil and water begin to flow. The oil must then be separated from the water, usually by centrifuge.

The finest oils come from the first light pressing accomplished mostly by the weight of the stacked mats themselves. As the pressure increases so does acidity, and quality decreases. These lesser oils are then refined — corrected for color, flavor, and acidity — before sale. The oil in the remains of the paste is extracted with the aid of solvents, then refined, resulting in an odorless, flavorless oil that is then blended with better oils for taste and sold as olive pomace oil.

Not all olive oils are pressed. To qualify as a virgin or extra-virgin olive oil, the oil must be produced by only mechanical or physical methods (no chemicals are allowed) and have a natural acidity below a specified level. Two other mechanical means are selective filtration (invented in 1911 in Spain) and centrifugation. Selective filtration works on the principal of oil's natural attraction to metal. Stainless steel plates are dipped into the paste, and the oil adheres to them; they are then lifted and drip oil into a receiving vessel.

In centrifugation, a heavy-duty decanting centrifuge swirls the paste, throwing oil and water in one direction and the solids in another. A second centrifuge immediately separates oil and water. Quickly separating the new oil from the water is very important as the oil can pick up "off" flavors if left too long in contact with the vegetative water.

Olive oil easily picks up flavors and aromas—an inconvenience and quality deterrent when too many leaves and stems are left with the olives when crushed or if the oil is not separated from its water fast enough. This vulnerability becomes an advantage when your interest is in making flavored (infused) oils.

One of the first uses of olive oil was as a flavored oil: Romans added aromatic substances to olive oil, which was almost always rancid because of the primitive extraction techniques, and used it cosmetically, rubbing it on their bodies as a moisturizer. Making what we know now as high-quality olive oil was not possible until early in the last century when "rectification" processes were developed. Once the olive oil is made, it is analyzed for acidity. Extra-virgin and virgin olive oils receive no further processing; oils with higher acidity levels are refined — corrected for color, aroma, and flavor to produce a clean, neutral-tasting oil. A percentage of virgin or extra-virgin olive oil is added to this neutral oil to give it flavor and it is sold simply as "olive oil."

Just before bottling, most olive oils are filtered to remove tiny olive particles and produce a brilliant, clear color. Some people prefer unfiltered olive oils, although it is very difficult to distinguish any differences in taste.

Olive oil grades are determined by acidity levels. Taste varies according to the "house style" of the producer. Virgin and extra-virgin oils will show variations according to vintage as well. Olive oil is actually a fruit juice, the juice of olives, and is therefore perishable. Look for bottling or harvest dates and buy oil as fresh as possible. Store it in a cool, dark place. Once opened, use within a relatively short time.

EXTRA VIRGIN OLIVE OIL AND VIRGIN OLIVE OIL

All virgin olive oil is extracted from olives only by mechanical means. The resulting oil must experience no treatments other than washing, decantation, centrifugation, and filtration. The oil's flavor must be without flaw. Two levels of virgin oil are sold in the United States: extra-virgin olive oil and virgin olive oil. The primary difference is their acidity level.

EXTRA-VIRGIN OLIVE OIL is the highest virgin oil quality grade. These oils have a distinctive taste ranging from soft and fruity to peppery depending on methods and timing of harvesting and handling as well as olive variety and specific growing conditions. The acidity is less than 1 percent.

VIRGIN OLIVE OIL also has individual taste characteristics though it is not as fine as extra-virgin olive oil. Its acidity varies from 1 to 3 percent.

OLIVE OIL (once called pure olive oil) is the name for a blend of refined olive oil and virgin olive oil. Some virgin oil is not considered edible without refining usually because its acidity is too high or it has taste flaws. Refining results in a clean, neutral-tasting oil. Typically, 5 to 10 percent or more virgin or extra-virgin olive oil is blended with the refined oil for flavor and balance.

OLIVE POMACE OIL is the least expensive oil. It is oil extracted with the use of solvents from the remains of the olive paste after extraction of olive oil by other means. This oil is then refined to produce a neutral oil and blended with virgin olive oil for flavor and body.

LIGHT OLIVE OIL is not a quality grade of olive oil nor does it have anything to do with calories. It is not "healthier" than any other olive oil. Instead, it is a marketing gimmick to describe the oil's flavor. "Light olive oil" is an olive oil blended for its "light" (neutral) taste. To me, it is nonsense to pay more for less. Try a "light" oil and a less expensive olive oil and see if you can tell the difference.

Whatever the quality grade or blend, *all olive oils are created equal in calories and fat grams*. Since olives are a fruit, they contain no cholesterol. The United States has defined a serving portion of olive oil as one tablespoon. One tablespoon contains 14 grams of fat and 120 calories, all of which are from fat. However, olive oil has proportionately very little harmful saturated fat, which raises blood cholesterol, and lots of the more beneficial monounsaturated and polyunsaturated fats. Olive oil is 77 percent monounsaturated fat, which has been shown to reduce low density lipoprotein (LDL—the kind of cholesterol you don't want) circulating in the blood while high density lipoprotein (HDL—the "good" cholesterol) levels remain unchanged.

I am often asked why I cook with extra-virgin olive oil for all types of cooking including sautéing. My questioners have been taught such use is a waste of expensive oil. My response is though some flavor is lost, the resulting dish will taste better than if a lower-quality oil were used. There are times, however, when extra-virgin oil is not appropriate. For instance, I use simple olive oil when the strong olive taste of an extra-virgin oil would interfere with a preparation, such as in a mayonnaise. For the same reason, I use simple olive oil when making flavored oils. For me, the point of flavored oils is that the oil carries the herbal flavor throughout a dish in a way that adding fresh herbs may not. I want the herbal flavor to dominate and the olive oil to be a supporting flavor.

If you look closely at Italian cooking, you will discover it is a cuisine of preservation, born of a necessity to conserve ingredients in season for eating out of season—grapes into wine, pork into prosciutto and pancetta, milk into cheese, tomatoes into sauce and dried tomatoes, olives into olive oil. Flavored oils in Italian cooking were not an end in themselves, they were a by-product of something else: the tomato-scented oil covering dried tomatoes, the aromatic oil preserving a harvest of wild mushrooms.

Making flavored oils for my Napa Valley restaurant, Tra Vigne, grew naturally out of my style of cooking. I think of my style as having three components—impeccable ingredients, solid technique, and a degree of fantasy. Flavored oils include all three aspects—intensely flavored herbs, the infusion technique, and color and versatility, which take them into the realm of fantasy. Whenever used, infused oils add these same dimensions to any dish. For instance, fresh mozzarella with vine-ripened tomato and basil is transformed by basil oil's intense aromas and brilliant green color. And esoteric flavors such as lavender (which is usually only seen in culinary use as part of *herbes de Provence* or sugared as a cake decoration) extracts wonderfully into olive oil and can then be used as a cooking ingredient. I mix it with honey and balsamic vinegar as a marinade for roasted salmon (page 87).

There are also technical reasons to cook with flavored oils. The role of oil and other fats in cooking is at least twofold: They add richness and "carry" flavor into a dish, increasing the amount of perceived flavor. Flavored oils make their intense flavors immediately available whether using mushroom, garlic, or rosemary. Fresh herbs cooked long enough in a dish to disperse their flavors will lose freshness. When added at the end of the cooking process, their effect often goes unnoticed. But flavored olive oils disperse their flavor throughout a dish immediately and maintain their fresh herbal flavor.

Flavored oils also can add depth and strength to your cooking with their versatility, flavor, and convenience. Use them, without plan, as a condiment: to drizzle on top of pasta, pizza, and bruschetta; to finish dishes by floating a spoonful in soups and sauces; or as a sauce "substitute" on meats and vegetables. As an ingredient, oils infused with fresh herbs substitute for the fresh herb. Dried herbs are not really an adequate substitute for fresh; their flavors are unto themselves. Recipes usually list dried herbs as a substitute for fresh (including recipes in this book) as a compromise only.

A few practical words of advice before you begin your explorations: Your flavored oils will only have as much flavor as the ingredients you use. I recommend using a simple olive oil so the herb or vegetable flavor of the infusion will dominate. Although amounts of flavoring ingredients are given, making flavored oils is not an exact science. Results depend on the freshness and flavor strength of the herbs, vegetables, and spices. Different varieties even of the same herb have varying intensities of flavor. Whether it is early, late, or the height of the season for the ingredients also affects flavor. Grow your own herbs, ask a friend, or go to farmers' markets and smell and taste the herbs before infusing them. If you use tired, old basil, for example, your flavored oil will also taste old and tired.

Make small batches of oil and refrigerate them to preserve their flavor. You will gain confidence faster with small batches — successful experiments can be repeated, unsuccessful ones forgotten. Use the oils within a week to take advantage of the freshness of their flavor. My style of cooking accentuates big, strong flavors. If you prefer more subtle flavors, cut down the amount of flavoring ingredients.

Following are several methods (with variations) for infusing flavors into olive oil. They are faster and result in stronger flavors than the traditional method of putting several sprigs of an herb in olive oil and waiting several weeks or a month before use. Use the cold method for delicate herbs such as basil, cilantro, and chervil, and a variation of that method for garlic.

The best method for making roasted garlic oil, in my opinion, is by roasting whole garlic heads in ample amounts of olive oil so you get both the rich-tasting paste and the flavored oil. Use the warm method for spices and for more resinous herbs including rosemary and oregano, and a variation of that method for chilies or mushrooms. I have developed another method for citrus. In Tuscany, occasionally whole lemons will be crushed with the whole olives into a paste and pressed so that the lemon becomes an integral part of the oil's flavor. It is a delicate process and the oils are very expensive. The results you will have with the method outlined here emphasize the fresh, juicy flavor of citrus. Orange works particularly well and I love it with beets and tomatoes. Just make sure the oranges are sweet, juicy, and have a just-picked aroma. I have had great luck with navel oranges.

Filtering the oils requires some degree of patience. This is especially true for the cold infusion method in which you purée the herb in the oil. For a filter, I have had the most luck with cheesecloth, which I rinse and squeeze dry first. But any cotton cloth will do — a sheet, clean rag, tea towel, napkin — as long as you rinse it well first to remove any smell or taste of detergent. For the warm infusion method, filter the oil while still warm; it goes much faster!

ROASTED GARLIC PASTE AND OIL

Serve roasted garlic hot from the oven with grilled bread and a salad or make a paste to spread on pizza or to mix by the spoonful into soups, stews, and sauces for extra flavor. To make roasted garlic oil, simply double the amount of oil.

1	pound whole garlic heads (6 to 8 whole heads garlic)
½	cup extra-virgin olive oil (use 1 cup for roasted garlic oil)
	Salt and freshly ground pepper

Preheat oven to 375 degrees F. Slice off top ⅓ of each head and discard or save for another use. Peel off outer layers of skin. Place close together in a shallow baking dish just large enough to hold the garlic. Pour oil over garlic and season amply with salt and pepper. Cover with aluminum foil and bake until cloves begin to pop out of their skins, about 1 hour. Uncover and bake another 15 minutes or until golden brown.

To make the paste, squeeze the garlic cloves into a bowl and mash. To store, cover with a thin layer of the olive oil in which it baked and refrigerate up to 2 days. Reserve baking oil in a tightly covered, sterilized glass jar or bottle and use within 1 week.

Makes about ¾ cup garlic paste and ⅓ cup roasted garlic oil; or ¾ cup roasted garlic oil if using 1 cup oil.

CHEF'S NOTES: *The roasted garlic-flavored baking oil is wonderful simply added to vinaigrettes, for sautéing vegetables, or in any of the recipes calling for roasted garlic oil.*

GARLIC FLAVORED OIL
Cold Infusion Method

Choose unblemished garlic without cracks or soft spots. For roasted garlic oil, see following recipe.

1	head raw garlic, separated into cloves and peeled (about ⅓ cup finely chopped)
½	cup distilled white vinegar
1	cup olive oil

Soak cloves in vinegar 15 minutes, drain, and rinse under cold, running water. Drain, dry well, then put in blender with oil and pulse until chopped. Do not blend to a purée or the oil and garlic will be too difficult to separate!

Strain purée immediately through a fine-mesh strainer such as a china cap. Strain again through 4 layers of cheesecloth and put in a sterilized glass bottle. Cover tightly and refrigerate. Use within 1 week for optimum flavor.

Makes about ¾ cup.

HERB FLAVORED OILS
Cold Infusion Method

For the best results, choose very fresh herbs with strong flavors and an olive oil with a clean, neutral taste. A blender makes a finer, smoother purée than a food processor and extracts more flavor. Some oil will be lost during filtering depending on how tightly it binds to the flavoring ingredients.

    2   cups tightly packed soft-leaved green herb
        (such as basil, chervil, chives, cilantro, mint)
    1   cup olive oil

Bring a large saucepan of water to a boil. Add herbs and make sure to push the leaves *under* the boiling water. Blanch herbs 5 seconds. Drain into a strainer and immediately plunge into a bowl of ice water. Drain well and squeeze out all liquid. Purée in a blender with olive oil.

Strain purée immediately through a fine-mesh strainer such as a china cap. Strain again through 4 layers of cheesecloth and put in a sterilized glass bottle. Cover tightly and refrigerate. Use within 1 week for optimum flavor.

Makes about ¾ cup.

CHEF'S NOTES: *Tarragon does not work very well except early in the spring when it is very sweet, otherwise it tends to taste bitter when infused.*

Make sure to squeeze all the water out of the cheesecloth or filter papers before use.

This method results in an oil that captures the fresh flavor of citrus. Look for fruit with thin skins—the more pith, the more bitter the flavor. If you can only find fruit with thick skins, see Chef's Notes. Orange is a knockout. Try tangerines and kumquats, too. You can also make an oil with both an orange and a lemon though I prefer the clear flavor of the single fruit.

    2   medium oranges *or* 3 lemons,
        Meyer lemons, or limes, cut in eighths
    1   cup olive oil

Roughly chop the fruit—skin, seeds and all—in a food processor with short pulses or use a chef's knife. Do *not* process to a purée. If the fruit is too finely chopped, the oil will emulsify with the pulp and not separate. Transfer the fruit to the work bowl of an electric mixer and add the oil. Mix on low speed 10 minutes with the paddle attachment. Let stand at room temperature 2 hours.

Rinse 4 layers of cheesecloth in cold water and squeeze dry. Suspend a fine-mesh strainer over a fat separator or bowl. Put the citrus mixture in the cheesecloth and squeeze to extract the oil. (As you squeeze, the web of cheesecloth loosens. The strainer will catch the bits of pulp which may escape.) Let stand again to allow oil and juice to separate. The clear oil will float above the thick mixture of juice, pulp, and some emulsified oil. Pour off oil into a sterilized glass jar or bottle and discard juice. Cover tightly, refrigerate, and use within 1 week.

Makes about ½ cup.

CHEF'S NOTES: *If lemons have thick skins, the pith may add some bitterness to the oil. To avoid this, peel the zest with a vegetable peeler, put in a food processor, and chop finely. Cut the pith off the fruit being careful not to cut into the pulp. You want to save as much juice and pulp as possible. Cut the fruit into eighths and process with the zest. Then put in a stand mixer and mix as above.*

Variation for Kumquats: Use ½ pound fruit for 1 cup oil and follow the method above. I have also seen limequats occasionally in the shops; they would make an intriguing oil. If you find them or grow them, be sure to try making a citrus oil with them.

DRIED MUSHROOM OR CHILI OIL
Warm Infusion Method

Experiment with combinations of dried, fresh, and smoked chilies to add different flavor dimensions to your oil, not just heat. Try fresh poblanos, jalapeños, and serranos or dried anchos and pasillas. Roast one of the fresh or dried chilies to add flavor. Add black pepper to the mix. It makes a truly amazing oil! Mushroom oil can be made from packaged, dried mushrooms such as porcini and shiitake. Mushroom hunters can dry their less than perfect specimens and use them for oil.

4	fresh hot chilies (unseeded) or 8 dried chilies (of a single type or mix for more complex flavors) or 1 ounce dried mushrooms such as porcini or shiitake
1	cup olive oil

Chop mushrooms or chilies in a food processor until fine. Place in a pot with the oil and heat until mixture begins to bubble. Let cook 10 to 15 seconds and remove from heat. Swirl until just warm. Strain into a bowl through 4 layers of cheesecloth. Squeeze well to extract as much oil as possible. Pour into a sterilized jar or bottle, seal tightly, refrigerate, and use within 1 week for best flavor.

Makes about ¾ cup mushroom oil; about 1 cup chili oil.

CHEF'S NOTES: *If you filter through coffee filters, rinse them and squeeze dry before use. You will need some patience and probably several filters. Pour the oil little by little and stir occasionally.*

You will recover almost all the oil if you use dried chilies; however, the more fresh chilies, the less chili oil since the oil will bind and be hard to separate after being infused.

HERB OR SPICE FLAVORED OILS
Warm Infusion Method

Use this method for tough-leafed herbs such as rosemary and sage as well as dried spices, or for dried mushrooms and fresh or dried chilies (see following recipe). Use the amounts of flavoring ingredients as a guide, feeling free to add more or less depending on the quality of your ingredients and your taste preferences. Dried spices extract very well and make delicious oils. For the best flavor, grind your own spices from the whole spice or buy a fresh supply of ground spices. The amount given below will make a strongly flavored oil; you can dilute with more olive oil if desired.

½	cup finely chopped fresh rosemary, sage, oregano, or lavender or ¾ cup (about 2 ounces) ground cumin, cinnamon, nutmeg, ginger, star anise, saffron, black pepper, or curry powder or ¼ cup chopped fresh ginger
1	cup olive oil

Put herbs or spices and oil in a heavy saucepan. Heat over high heat until mixture begins to sizzle gently. Let cook about 10 seconds, remove pan from heat, and swirl contents until sizzling stops. Pour through a fine strainer or coffee filters into a sterilized bottle or jar. Press down on herbs to release last bit of oil and flavor. Seal tightly, refrigerate, and use within 1 week for best flavor.

Makes about 1 cup.

Flavored oils can add incredible versatility to any cook's repertoire. Once made, they shorten preparation time— no more picking fresh herbs from their stems and then mincing. And they add their flavor to a dish more evenly and rapidly than adding finely chopped fresh herbs.

Practicality, however, is not the best reason to buy or make flavored oils. The best reason is their own intense flavor and the creative potential they represent. One sniff of rosemary oil and a cook may recall the pan of tiny roasted potatoes with rosemary at a shop in a small, Italian coastal town. The fresh, summer smell of basil oil calls for plunging into — with raw or cooked vegetables, or just a piece of bread.

Suddenly, a cook — with several flavored oils on hand — has many options available to transform even standard recipes. Instead of reaching for olive oil to sauté garlic, reach for roasted garlic oil and go directly to adding vegetables such as spinach or broccoli. With a pinch of red pepper flakes or a spoonful of pepper oil to finish, you have a delicious dish to serve alongside chicken or to use as a pasta sauce. Don't feel guilty that cooking can be so easy, just enjoy it!

The recipes in this book are organized by flavor. However, each recipe will produce delicious results with extra-virgin or virgin olive oil and fresh herbs. Most of the recipes may also be varied themselves by substituting a different flavored oil than the one called for. Or try combining two oils with compatible flavors — rosemary and orange, for example — in a single dish. Following are some hints for using flavored oils in your cooking.

☺ *Flavored oils are a cholesterol-free butter substitute. Dip bread into them or drizzle on toasted or grilled bread and any kind of potatoes, rice, polenta, or pasta. Dip bread sticks in flavored oil or brush them with rosemary, roasted garlic, or pepper oil before baking. Brush flavored oils on focaccia before baking or use flavored oils to give fresh flavor to commercial, prebaked pizza shells such as Boboli and even to drizzle on frozen or take-out pizza!*

Toss croutons with flavored oils and use them in salads and soups.

☺ *Mix dried bread crumbs with garlic and rosemary oils, and toast in the oven until golden. Add grated Parmesan and fontina cheeses and use for gratins.*

☺ *Vinaigrettes, dressings, and marinades can be varied enormously by using flavored oils. A simple salad of mixed greens shows off the virtuosity of flavored oils. Use a citrus oil alone (no vinegar) to dress a salad, especially if you are serving good wines with your meal. Dressings make delicious sauces for fish, meats, and vegetables. There are several throughout this book.*

☺ *Dress up simple, fresh cheeses such as mozzarella and goat cheese by marinating them in flavored oils. This can be as simple as pouring a spoonful of oil over the cheese just before serving or leaving the two together for a day before serving.*

☺ *Give soup (homemade, frozen, or canned) a taste perk with a flavored oil. Add oils to various tomato sauces.*

☺ *Drizzle tomatoes with flavored oil before oven-drying them.*

☺ *Make Hollandaise sauce with warmed flavored oils instead of clarified butter.*

☺ *Fry eggs and home fries in pepper oil and serve them with grilled or toasted bread brushed with roasted garlic oil.*

☺ *Roast whole heads of garlic in rosemary or pepper oil to give both the garlic and the resulting oil an intriguing new flavor.*

☺ *Only a few flavored oils will stand up to high heat or even to low heat of long duration. The delicate flavors, especially those of basil and cilantro, will evaporate as they would if you exposed the raw ingredients to the same treatment. Some, such as rosemary, porcini, roasted garlic, and pepper oils, are sturdier. Roasted garlic, for instance, is already cooked; rosemary's resinous character makes it more resistant to high heat; and cooking will not destroy the heat of chilies though it may affect nuances of flavor. The flavor of porcini oil seems to become deeper and sweeter with heat. If you do choose to expose flavored oils to high heat, do so quickly, then add other ingredients to buffer the effect and add more flavored oil to finish the dish with a fresher flavor.*

☺ *Store homemade flavored oils in clean glass jars and bottles and use within a week. Unopened commercial flavored oils should be stored in a cool, dark place and refrigerated once opened. They should be used within a month.*

Basil olive oil was the first infused oil I made. I worked backwards from pesto, taking out the cheese and nuts to make an olive oil and herb slurry. We used these slurries in the restaurant to great advantage and still use them: We make a tarragon slurry because tarragon, except for early in the season when it is very sweet, does not infuse well. Herbs, even when blanched first to set their color, can look dark and unattractive. The oil of the slurry, however, turned a beautiful, jeweled green color, so we began filtering the herbs out of the oil.

We started making the basil oil for our shop, the Cantinetta, just across the courtyard from the Tra Vigne restaurant. We set the oil out with small cubes of bread so people could taste it, and soon I was hunting for basil growers who could grow basil in the amount and with the intensity needed to make the strongly aromatic oil.

Basil is probably the most popular flavor for an infused oil and with good reason — all the things loved best about summer are concentrated in its aroma. I love basil oil simply for dipping bread or raw vegetables and for drizzling over vine-ripened tomatoes. But do not subject basil oil to high heat; you will lose a good deal of its flavor. And now you can enjoy pesto year round without using all your freezer space. Basil oil is the secret with parsley masquerading as basil.

BASIL DRESSING

The additions of roasted red pepper and olive paste give this vinaigrette the substance to dress vegetable and pasta salads served slightly warm or at room temperature.

½	cup plus 1 teaspoon basil olive oil (page 22)
1	teaspoon finely chopped garlic
1	tablespoon finely diced roasted red pepper (page 93)
2	tablespoons fresh lemon juice (preferably from Meyer lemons)
1	teaspoon black olive paste or tapenade (see Chef's Notes)
	Salt and freshly ground pepper

Heat the 1 teaspoon basil oil in a small sauté pan over medium heat. Add garlic and cook slowly until transparent, about 2 minutes. Add roasted peppers and stir. Add lemon juice and mix well. Add remaining basil oil and olive paste and mix well again. Add salt and pepper to taste and remove from heat and let rest 1 to 2 minutes before mixing with a salad or pasta.

Makes about ½ cup.

CHEF'S NOTES: *Olive paste and tapenade may both be made at home from whole black olives or purchased. Olive paste is a rough purée of olives; tapenade is also a purée of olives but flavored with anchovy and other seasonings.*

BALSAMIC BASIL VINAIGRETTE

This is a delicious all-purpose vinaigrette. Use it for any green salad, for vegetable salads such as grilled or roasted eggplant, and for main-dish salads such as green lentils and chicken. The recipe may be doubled.

¼	cup balsamic vinegar
1	teaspoon finely chopped garlic
2	teaspoons finely chopped shallots
1	cup basil olive oil (page 22)
	Salt and freshly ground pepper

Whisk together vinegar, garlic, and shallots in a small bowl. Whisk in basil oil and season to taste with salt and pepper. Keeps up to 4 days refrigerated in a tightly sealed container.

Makes about 1¼ cups.

CHEF'S NOTES: *Balsamic vinegar can vary greatly in quality and strength. This recipe was written for less expensive vinegar. If you use an aged balsamic, you might want to reduce the quantity.*

BASIL MARINADE

This basic marinade gives poultry and fish an aromatic flavor without masking their own delicate flavors. It is also good for marinating vegetables before roasting or grilling.

½	cup basil olive oil (page 22)
1½	teaspoons finely chopped garlic
½	small yellow onion, roughly chopped
2	tablespoons chopped fresh tarragon
	or 2 teaspoons dried tarragon
	(rehydrated, see Chef's Notes)
¼	cup dry white wine

Put all ingredients in a food processor or blender and process 20 seconds. Place poultry or fish in a nonreactive dish and pour marinade over it. Cover, refrigerate, and let marinate — depending on the size of what is being cooked — 15 minutes for thin fillets, 3 hours for chicken pieces.

When ready to cook, remove from marinade and cook to desired doneness. Discard marinade.

Makes about 1 cup.

CHEF'S NOTES: *To release the flavor of the dried tarragon, rehydrate it by mixing it with the white wine and let stand a few minutes before adding to the marinade.*

BASIL OIL PESTO

Basil Oil Pesto has innumerable uses — as a sauce for pasta and pizza, as a sandwich spread, a sauce for grilled or roasted meats, poultry and fish, and even as a flavorful addition to soups and stews.

2	large bunches fresh flat-leaf parsley
1	cup basil olive oil (page 22)
1	tablespoon finely chopped garlic or
	½ tablespoon roasted
	garlic olive oil (page 21)
2	tablespoons lightly toasted pine nuts
	(see Chef's Notes)
5	tablespoons freshly grated
	Parmesan cheese
	Salt and freshly ground pepper

Remove tough stems from parsley and discard. Blanch parsley very quickly in rapidly boiling, salted water to brighten and stabilize the color. Plunge immediately in a bowl of ice water to stop the cooking, then drain well and squeeze out excess water.

Spread parsley on a cutting board and roughly chop it. Place it in a blender and add remaining ingredients except Parmesan cheese, salt, and pepper; blend until smooth. Pulse in Parmesan. Season with salt and pepper to taste. Sauce keeps up to 2 days, refrigerated, in a tightly sealed container. May also be frozen.

Makes about 1½ cups.

CHEF'S NOTES: *Put pine nuts on a baking sheet or in a small baking pan and toast in a preheated 350 degree F oven about 5 minutes or until brown. Stir once or twice, or shake the pan, to ensure even browning. Watch carefully as pine nuts burn easily. They may also be toasted in a small skillet over medium heat.*

PASTA WITH TOMATO VINAIGRETTE

This is my favorite summer pasta. Every Sunday morning my daughters and I go into the garden and pick whatever is at its freshest and ripest and incorporate it into this tomato vinaigrette. We especially like sautéed zucchini, grilled eggplant, and roasted peppers. Paired with a chilled sauvignon blanc, the dish makes a complete summer supper and the kitchen stays clean and cool. The idea of cooking in the summer is to free yourself to spend time with family and friends!

8	medium vine-ripened red tomatoes, peeled, seeded, and finely chopped
2	tablespoons minced shallots
1	tablespoon minced garlic
6	tablespoons finely chopped fresh flat-leaf parsley
¼	cup fresh lemon juice (preferably from Meyer lemons)
1	cup basil olive oil (page 22) Salt and freshly ground pepper
1½	pounds dried pasta (such as rigatoni or orecchiette)
1	cup freshly grated Parmesan or pecorino cheese

Mix together tomatoes, shallots, garlic, ¼ cup of the parsley, lemon juice, basil oil, and salt and pepper to taste in a nonaluminum bowl and let rest at room temperature 15 to 20 minutes to let flavors develop. If making further ahead, do not salt until 15 minutes before serving, otherwise salt will draw all the water out of the tomatoes.

When ready to eat, bring a large pot of salted water to the boil and cook pasta until al dente. Drain well and toss with tomato vinaigrette. Add ½ cup cheese and mix well. Garnish each serving with additional cheese and parsley. Serve immediately.

Serves 6.

CHEF'S NOTES: *This pasta is meant to be served just slightly warm, just above room temperature. If you would like it warmer, place the bowl of tomato vinaigrette over the pasta pot while the pasta is cooking to let the steam warm it.*

The pasta shape is important: rigatoni and orecchiette ("little ears" or small shells) both hold the sauce. If you choose a smooth, straight shape such as spaghetti, the sauce will drain off into a pool at the bottom of the bowl. We also like cappellini for this dish. It holds the sauce very well but everyone must be ready to sit down and eat immediately when it is done!

THE PLT — PANCETTA, LETTUCE, AND TOMATO SANDWICH

At the Cantinetta, in the corner of Tra Vigne's courtyard, we make this sandwich with a sandwich press. When I tested it at home, I used our waffle iron with the flat plates inserted. The bread is buttered on the outside and grilled with only the pancetta inside. When the bread is toasted, separate the sandwich, spread the basil mayonnaise on one side, add the remaining ingredients, then reassemble.

6	ounces pancetta, cut into ¼-inch pieces
2	tablespoons unsalted butter, softened
8	slices rustic bread (such as crusty Italian bread) cut about ⅜-inch thick
2-3	vine-ripened tomatoes, sliced ¼-inch thick
4	tablespoons Basil-Garlic Mayonnaise About 3 cups loosely packed arugula Salt and freshly ground pepper

Cook pancetta in a skillet until crisp and drain on paper towels. Spread butter on one side of bread. Divide pancetta among 4 slices on the unbuttered side. Top with second slice, buttered side up. Put in a preheated sandwich press, a waffle iron fitted with flat plates, or a skillet placed over medium heat. If you use a skillet, press down firmly on the sandwich with a spatula. Cook until brown on one side, then turn and toast second side.

Separate sandwich halves and arrange tomato slices on top of pancetta. Spread each other half with 1 tablespoon basil mayonnaise. Add arugula and season with salt and pepper to taste. Close sandwiches and cut in half. Serve immediately.

Makes 4 sandwiches.

CHEF'S NOTES: *For a more sophisticated flavor and presentation, use brioche baked in a square pain de mie pan or loaf shape.*

If the pancetta you buy is very fatty, you may want to buy a little more since it will lose so much volume when cooked.

BASIL-GARLIC MAYONNAISE

This is a basic mayonnaise which can be made with any flavored oil. If you want to make it without a flavored oil, use olive oil or a vegetable oil. Extra-virgin olive oil has too strong a flavor for mayonnaise. I like a little garlic in mayonnaise. If you don't, leave it out. Also, if you are concerned about using raw eggs, see variation at end of recipe.

1	clove garlic, finely chopped
1	egg yolk
2	teaspoons champagne wine vinegar or freshly squeezed lemon juice
¾	cup basil olive oil (page 22) Salt and freshly ground pepper
2	tablespoons finely chopped fresh basil (optional)

Whisk garlic with egg yolk and vinegar in a bowl or process in a food processor or blender. Start whisking in the basil oil, drop by drop, to form an emulsion. If using a machine, add oil little by little with the machine running. As mixture forms an emulsion, add remaining oil in a slow, steady stream while whisking or processing continuously. Season to taste with salt and pepper and stir in chopped basil, if using. If a thinner consistency is desired, whisk in a little warm water, 1 teaspoon at a time.

Makes about ¾ cup.

Variation with Pasteurized Liquid Eggs and Cholesterol-Free Liquid Eggs: Follow directions on the package and use the equivalent of one whole egg for the mayonnaise recipes in this book. Cholesterol-free liquid eggs, such as Egg Beaters, are readily available and work for these recipes as well. Use ¼ cup liquid egg and 1 tablespoon vinegar or lemon juice and proceed with the recipe as written. The texture is very light but the emulsion does not break and it tastes very good. There is the added benefit of enjoying mayonnaise without fear of cholesterol!

CHEF'S NOTES: *If sauce breaks (separates), start again with another yolk and add the broken sauce teaspoon by teaspoon, whisking all the while (or processing) to form an emulsion. As emulsion forms, drizzle in remainder.*

GRILLED HALIBUT WITH BASIL-ORANGE MARINADE

Reducing the orange juice intensifies its flavor and lessens the acidity. This allows marinating the fish without "cold" cooking it as in a ceviche. Serve the fish with a salad of thinly sliced fennel and red onions tossed with salt and pepper, basil oil, and unreduced orange juice.

1½	cups fresh orange juice
1	bay leaf
8	whole black peppercorns
½	cup basil olive oil (page 22)
2	pounds halibut fillets, cut into 4 equal pieces
	Salt and freshly ground pepper

Strain orange juice through a fine sieve into a non-aluminum saucepan. Add bay leaf and peppercorns and bring to a boil. Simmer until reduced to ½ cup and let cool. Remove and discard bay leaf and peppercorns. Slowly whisk in basil oil to form an emulsion.

Preheat grill or broiler. Put fish in a flat glass or enamel dish and pour ½ the marinade over the fish. Turn fish several times to coat evenly with marinade. Cover, refrigerate, and marinate at least 1 hour. Drain fish and discard used marinade. Season with salt and pepper. Grill until done, about 10 minutes per inch of thickness, depending on heat of the grill. When half cooked, turn and brush with some of the remaining marinade. Continue to grill until done. Serve immediately with remaining marinade as a sauce.

Serves 4.

CHEF'S NOTES: *Be sure to liberally oil the grill or the fish will stick, or invest in a nonstick or cast iron insert for the barbecue.*

Depending on the thickness of the fish, it can be marinated for longer than an hour and up to 6 to 8 hours.

PESTO PIZZA WITH ROASTED GARLIC AND TOMATO

What could possibly be better on a hot summer day than a freshly made pizza redolent with the aromas of summer? Serve with a glass of sauvignon blanc or pinot bianco. The flavor of this pizza insists on great tomatoes. Arrange the tomatoes to cover the entire pizza so the tomato flavor will be part of every bite.

	Pizza Dough (page 36)
½	cup Roasted Garlic Paste (page 21)
½	cup Basil Oil Pesto (page 30)
	Coarse cornmeal, for baking sheet
4-5	large, vine-ripened tomatoes, of any color or variety, sliced ⅛-inch thick
	Salt and freshly ground pepper
1	cup freshly grated Parmesan cheese

Preheat oven to 500 degrees F. Place baking sheet in oven to preheat.

Shape ⅓ of pizza dough into a 10-inch circle on a lightly floured board. Spread with ⅓ of the garlic paste. Be sure to spread to within a half-inch of the edge (see Chef's Notes). Sprinkle ⅓ of the pesto on dough and spread out smoothly on top of garlic paste.

Remove baking sheet from oven and sprinkle with cornmeal. Transfer pizza to baking sheet and put in oven. Bake until light brown and bubbling, about 10 minutes. Remove pizza from oven and quickly arrange sliced tomatoes on top. Do not overlap slices. Season with salt and pepper to taste. Sprinkle with ⅓ of the Parmesan cheese and return pizza to oven another 2 to 3 minutes or until cheese melts. Immediately transfer to a board, cut, and serve. Repeat for remaining two pizzas.

Makes three 10-inch pizzas; or serves 6 as supper with a salad.

CHEF'S NOTES: *One of my pet peeves is pizza topping not spread close to the edge of the dough. This means that all the filling is eaten in the first and second bites, leaving only crust for the last. Not to mention a slice that will not hold straight when picked up!*

PIZZA DOUGH

The recipe can be doubled if you would prefer a thicker crust than recommended here. To ensure a really crisp crust, bake the crust "blond" first (without any topping) until light brown. My mother would do this, baking the crust ahead of time. Then when I came in and was ready to eat, she would add tomato sauce and cheese and put it back in the oven. You might think flavored oils in the dough would give subtle variations; instead their flavor gets lost. Save the flavored oils to top the pizzas.

1	cake (0.6 ounce) fresh yeast or 1 package active dry yeast
½	cup lukewarm water
3½	cups all-purpose flour plus additional flour for kneading
½	cup whole wheat flour
1	cup water
2	tablespoons extra-virgin olive oil plus additional oil for brushing bowl and dough
2	teaspoons salt
	Coarse cornmeal, for baking sheet

Combine yeast, the warm water, and ½ cup of the flour in the bowl of an electric mixer. Let stand 15 minutes to activate yeast. Add the remaining 3 cups all-purpose flour, whole wheat flour, the 1 cup water, olive oil, and salt. Mix with the dough hook attachment on low, then increase speed to medium low until the dough comes away from the bottom of the bowl. Dough should be slightly moist. Knead another minute.

Turn dough out onto a lightly floured surface and knead gently until smooth, folding the dough over itself. Shape into a ball, flatten into a fat disc with the heel of your hand, and put in an oiled bowl. Cover with a damp towel and let rise in a warm place until doubled in bulk, about 1 hour. Punch down and cut into 3 equal pieces. Roll each into a ball. Dough may be frozen at this point (see Chef's Notes). Brush lightly with olive oil and let rise in a warm place, covered, in oiled bowls or on a floured board, until doubled in size, about 30 minutes.

When ready to bake, preheat oven to 500 degrees F. On a lightly floured surface, flatten ball into a disc and nudge the dough outward into a circle with your fingers (see Chef's Notes). Flour the dough and the board as needed. Pick up the dough and, holding it by the edge, feed the circle through your fingers. Let the dough hang from your fingers onto the board. It will stretch as you work around the edges.

Lay dough back down on board and nudge into shape. If it needs further stretching, drape it over the backs of your closed fists. (Try this even if you do not feel as dexterous as the man in the pizza parlor!) Pull your fists gently apart from each other so that you rotate and stretch the dough. Return the dough to floured board and nudge into place. It should be about ⅛ inch thick and about 10 inches in diameter. If dough tears, simply press torn edges together firmly. The irregularities of hand-shaping are part of the charm.

Put baking sheet in the oven to preheat. When hot, remove, sprinkle with coarse cornmeal, and transfer dough onto it. Top as specified in recipe. Bake in the hot oven about 10 minutes or until crust is brown and crisp. Repeat with remaining dough.

Makes about 2 pounds dough, enough for three 10-inch pizzas.

CHEF'S NOTES: *If you freeze the pizza dough, defrost and let rise in the refrigerator. It triples and quadruples in volume with this method so be sure to use a large bowl and watch carefully that it does not overflow.*

You can roll out the dough with a rolling pin but this presses all the air out of the edges and creates a very flat pizza. Toppings that are slightly liquid, such as tomato sauce, or that melt, such as mozzarella, will leak off and spill.

TAELLA — SUMMER VEGETABLE GRATIN

Taella is the Italian name for a low, shallow baking dish. In my family, we would say, "Please pass the taella" when at the table. The name eventually came to mean this particular dish baked in the taella pan. You may also wish to serve this gratin spread on small toasts as an appetizer or use it to stuff ravioli.

¾ cup extra-virgin olive oil
1 yellow zucchini or yellow crookneck squash (about ½ pound), sliced into rounds ¼-inch thick
1 green zucchini (about ½ pound), sliced into rounds ¼-inch thick
   Salt and freshly ground pepper
2 tablespoons chopped fresh thyme or 2 teaspoons dried thyme
1 large red bell pepper, seeded and cut into ¼-inch dice
½ pound green beans, cut diagonally into ¼-inch pieces
6 ounces fresh wild or domestic mushrooms, sliced ¼-inch thick
1 large yellow onion, chopped
2 tablespoons finely chopped garlic
2 cups vine-ripened tomatoes, peeled, seeded, and chopped or good quality, canned plum (Roma) tomatoes
¼ cup basil olive oil (page 22)
½ cup freshly grated Parmesan cheese
1 cup dried bread crumbs (optional)

In a large sauté pan, heat 2 tablespoons of the extra-virgin olive oil over medium-high heat until it almost smokes. Add yellow and green zucchini and quickly sauté over high heat until zucchini just begins to color, about 5 minutes. Add salt, pepper, and a pinch thyme. Pour onto a baking sheet to cool.

Repeat cooking process with peppers, green beans, mushrooms, and onion, wiping out pan and adding 2 tablespoons fresh extra-virgin olive oil for each vegetable. Mushrooms and onion will take longer to brown because of their water and sugar content.

Heat remaining 2 tablespoons extra-virgin olive oil in a saucepan over medium-high heat. Add garlic and sauté quickly until light brown, about 1 minute. With a slotted spoon, take out half the garlic and put on top of the vegetables. Add the tomatoes to the saucepan and simmer until mixture thickens, 7 to 8 minutes. Add basil oil and then add salt and pepper to taste. Spread tomato mixture on a baking sheet to cool.

If planning to add the bread crumb topping, preheat oven to 450 degrees F. When all vegetables and tomatoes have cooled, gently toss together in a bowl and fold in ¼ cup of the Parmesan. Adjust seasoning as needed. At this point, the vegetables may be eaten as is or transfered to a baking dish for topping. Mix the bread crumbs with the remaining ¼ cup Parmesan and sprinkle evenly over the top. Bake until lightly browned, about 15 minutes. Serve warm.

Serves 6.

Oregano
Olive Oil

Oregano enhances so many different foods that it is one of the most important herbs in an Italian kitchen. Americans use the dried version frequently, especially in pizza parlors, but use fresh oregano much less frequently. In a pot or the garden, it grows easily and abundantly. Clip the fast-growing tips that appear to have bolted for making flavored olive oil. These have the most intense flavor.

Despite their differences in flavor, oregano oil and basil oil are nearly interchangeable because of their uses in cooking. They are often combined though I prefer to use one or the other. Try using oregano oil with citrus oil for summer cooking.

Oregano (and cilantro and even rosemary) can have a soapy quality to its flavor which does not appear when oregano is properly infused into oil. You can then intensify the herbal flavor of oregano without any side effects! Tomatoes and oregano taste especially good together. I have included an all-purpose tomato sauce and given variations in ingredients so it can be made summer and winter.

SUMMER/WINTER TOMATO SAUCE

This is a chunky, basic tomato sauce to use in lasagna, on pizza, for pasta. And it can even be made into a soup (see variations). There was a time when fresh tomatoes contained lots of acidity and needed long cooking and/or the addition of a spoonful of sugar to balance the acid. Today, the acid has for the most part been bred out of tomatoes. The good news is that you can make tomato sauce in a short time; the bad news is that it can lack flavor. I add sun-dried tomatoes for extra flavor and work with local growers to grow antique tomato varieties that have the flavor I remember from childhood. You can grow your own tomatoes or shop at farmers' markets where you are often allowed to taste before buying. Many markets now feature vine-ripened local tomatoes in season. Lacking tasty fresh tomatoes, use good quality canned tomatoes.

10	large tomatoes (about 4 pounds), peeled, seeded, and chopped or 2 cans (28 ounces each) high quality plum (Roma) tomatoes
2	tablespoons extra-virgin olive oil
2	tablespoons finely chopped garlic
1	bay leaf
¼-½	cup chopped sun-dried tomatoes packed in oil (use larger amount with canned tomatoes or to enhance fresh tomatoes lacking in flavor) Salt and freshly ground pepper
2	tablespoons unsalted butter
6	tablespoons oregano olive oil (page 24)

Reserve juice from the chopped, fresh tomatoes by putting them in a strainer over a bowl. If using canned tomatoes, strain the juice from the tomatoes; reserve juice and chop tomatoes.

In a large, heavy saucepan, heat the extra-virgin olive oil over medium-high heat until hot. Add garlic and sauté until lightly browned. Add tomato juice and bay leaf and increase heat to high. Simmer until the juice has reduced by ⅓ for canned tomatoes and until it is thick for fresh tomatoes. Add tomato solids and sun-dried tomatoes and simmer until excess liquid has evaporated, 15 to 20 minutes. Season to taste with salt and pepper. Just before serving, swirl in butter and oregano oil.

Makes about 4 cups.

CHEF'S NOTES: *If not using the tomato sauce immediately, do not finish with the butter and oregano oil. During cooking and reheating, the butter and oil will separate from the sauce. Instead, wait until you plan to use the sauce, then finish with butter and oil.*

Variation for a Smooth Sauce: To make a rich, smooth sauce which really adheres to pasta, put sauce in blender and blend until smooth. With machine running, add another cup of extra-virgin olive oil. Try the sauce with ravioli and cappellini.

Variation for Tomato Soup: Add 2 stalks celery (no leaves), chopped, and 1 medium onion, chopped, to the garlic and sauté until soft. Thin the sauce into a soup with chicken stock and finish with a little cream.

RIGATONI WITH WHITE BEANS AND ROASTED PEPPERS

The combination of beans and pasta makes this dish true comfort food. In winter, serve it warm sprinkled generously with freshly grated Parmesan and drizzled with oregano olive oil. In summer, serve it cool piled on top of ripe tomato slices.

WHITE BEANS

1	cup dried cannellini beans (see Glossary)
2	cups chicken stock (page 44) or canned, low-salt chicken broth
½	small onion
½	carrot
1	stalk celery
1	bay leaf
	Several prosciutto scraps (optional)
	Salt and freshly ground pepper

ROASTED PEPPER SAUCE AND PASTA

2	tablespoons extra-virgin olive oil
8	cloves garlic, thinly sliced
1	cup finely chopped yellow onion
2	teaspoons red pepper flakes
6	tablespoons oregano olive oil (page 24)
3½	tablespoons finely chopped fresh flat-leaf parsley
1	pound dried rigatoni pasta
2	red bell peppers, roasted, peeled, seeded, and julienned (page 93)
2	yellow bell peppers, roasted, peeled, seeded and julienned (page 93)
1½	cups freshly grated Parmesan or pecorino cheese
	Salt and freshly ground pepper

Put cannellini beans in a large saucepan with 4 cups cold water and bring to a boil over high heat. Cover and let stand until tepid, about 1 hour. Drain and rinse beans and return them to the pan with 2 cups water, chicken stock, onion, carrot, celery, bay leaf, and prosciutto. Bring to a boil over high heat; then lower heat and simmer very slowly until beans are tender, 1 to 1½ hours depending on the size and age of the beans. Season with salt and pepper to taste 15 minutes before beans are done. Reserve beans and their cooking liquid. Discard vegetables.

Heat extra-virgin olive oil in a large saucepan over medium heat until hot. Add garlic, onion, and red pepper flakes and sauté over medium-low heat until onions are soft and translucent, 3 to 5 minutes. Add beans and their cooking liquid and simmer a few minutes to blend flavors. Add 4 tablespoons of the oregano oil and 2 tablespoons of the parsley. Mix well.

Meanwhile, bring a large pot of salted water to a boil and add pasta. Cook until al dente, drain and rinse. (Can be cooked ahead of time; see Chef's Notes.)

Add cooked pasta to beans in saucepan with roasted red and yellow peppers and heat through. Stir in 1 cup of the cheese and season to taste with salt and pepper. Pour onto a heated platter or into a heated serving bowl and sprinkle with remaining ½ cup cheese and 1½ tablespoons parsley. Drizzle last 2 tablespoons oregano olive oil over all.

Serves 6.

CHEF'S NOTES: *If you cook the pasta ahead of time, toss it with 1 to 2 tablespoons oil so it will not get gummy and stick together. Submerge in boiling water 10 seconds to reheat before adding to dish.*

CHICKEN STOCK

I use "blond" chicken stock in the summer when my cooking is lighter in flavor to allow the fresh taste of bright summer vegetables to shine through. I like the richer, more caramelized flavors of brown chicken stock for fall and winter cooking.

5	pounds chicken bones (fresh, if possible, not frozen)
½	pound roughly chopped onions
¼	pound roughly chopped carrots
¼	pound roughly chopped celery (do not include leaves which give a bitter flavor)
2	bay leaves
6	whole black peppercorns
6	whole juniper berries (optional)
6	sprigs fresh flat-leaf parsley (optional)
6	sprigs fresh thyme (optional)

Rinse bones with cold water, put in a stockpot or large saucepan, and cover with cold water. Let rest 10 minutes, then drain and rinse again. (This washes off the blood and allows a clearer stock.) Return chicken bones to the stockpot and cover with cold water by an inch. Bring to a boil, reduce heat, and simmer 30 minutes. Skim foam from surface frequently. Continue to skim until mixture stops foaming.

Add onions, carrots, celery, bay leaves, peppercorns, and juniper berries, if using. Simmer very slowly another 4 hours. If using parsley and thyme, add only for last 30 minutes of cooking. Strain stock into a bowl, discard bones and vegetables. Cover and refrigerate stock until fat rises to surface and hardens. Discard fat and refrigerate or freeze. Stock keeps, refrigerated in a tightly sealed container, about 3 days.

Makes 4 cups.

Variation for Brown Chicken Stock: Preheat oven to 450 degrees F. After rinsing and soaking bones put them in a roasting pan, put in oven, and roast until brown all over. Stir bones occasionally. When browned, put bones in a stockpot and follow method above. While stock is simmering, put vegetables in the roasting pan and brown in the oven. When brown, transfer vegetables to stockpot. Immediately put roasting pan over medium heat and add about ½ cup red wine or water. Deglaze pan, scraping up all the brown bits which cling to the sides and bottom of the pan. Add to the stock and continue as above.

CHEF'S NOTES: *May be doubled and frozen.*

SPIEDINI OF PRAWNS WITH PANCETTA AND OREGANO DRESSING

The garlic and oregano dressing is served warm, so make it just before serving. Grilling the prawns over wood adds a wonderful flavor but they can also be broiled or even sautéed in a few tablespoons of oil. Serve the prawns with a cucumber, red onion, and yogurt salad.

2	pounds large prawns with shells (size 16/20 or larger, see Chef's Notes), peeled and deveined
36	(about) very thin slices pancetta
6	bamboo skewers, soaked, or metal skewers
2	tablespoons extra-virgin olive oil
1	large head garlic, separated into cloves and peeled
3	scallions
1	small red bell pepper, seeded, and cut into ¼-inch dice
2	tablespoons finely chopped fresh flat-leaf parsley
¼	cup sherry vinegar
¾	cup oregano olive oil (page 24) Salt and freshly ground pepper

Preheat grill or broiler. Wrap each prawn in a slice of pancetta. Thread wrapped prawns on skewers, about 5 or 6 per serving, and set aside until ready to cook.

Heat extra-virgin olive oil in a heavy saucepan until almost smoking. Add garlic cloves and "roast" until golden brown, 3 to 5 minutes. Watch them carefully so they do not burn. Remove smaller cloves as they brown or they will overcook. Let garlic cloves cool in their cooking oil. Strain, reserving oil and cloves separately. (Taste the oil. If it is not scorched-tasting, save it to add to marinades, vinaigrettes, etc.) Drain cloves on paper towel; then slice thinly.

To make the vinaigrette, slice scallions on the diagonal as thinly as possible using all the white parts and a little of the green. Put scallions and sliced garlic in a bowl with red pepper, parsley, vinegar, and oregano oil. Season to taste with salt and pepper.

Grill prawns until the pancetta is golden and prawns are cooked through, about 5 minutes depending on the heat of the grill. Turn once during cooking. To serve, spoon vinaigrette over prawns. Serve hot.

Serves 6 as an entrée (about 6 prawns per person).

CHEF'S NOTES: *Prawns are sized by the average number found in 1 pound. Therefore, 16/20s means there are between 16 and 20 prawns per pound.*

PAPPA AL POMODORO—
TOMATO AND BREAD SOUP WITH
OREGANO CROUTONS

This version of the classic Tuscan tomato and bread soup has more texture than the traditional recipe. I made it one summer when I thought my family and I could eat the production of six tomato plants. It is a soup to be made in the height of tomato season and no other time: July, August, and early September; not June and not October!

SOUP

3	pounds vine-ripened red tomatoes
3	tablespoons extra-virgin olive oil
	Salt and freshly ground pepper
2	tablespoons finely chopped garlic
1	tablespoon tomato paste
¼	cup oregano olive oil (page 24)

OREGANO CROUTONS

2	cups ½-inch bread cubes cut from crusty Italian bread
2	tablespoons oregano olive oil (page 24)
2	tablespoons freshly grated Parmesan cheese
	Salt and freshly ground pepper

GARNISH

2	bunches arugula
2	teaspoons freshly squeezed lemon juice
3	tablespoons oregano olive oil (page 24)
	Salt and freshly ground pepper

Preheat grill or broiler. Use your hands to lightly oil the tomatoes with 1 tablespoon of the extra-virgin olive oil and season with salt and pepper. Place on grill or under broiler until softened and skins have darkened and blistered. Do *not* cook tomatoes all the way through. Let tomatoes cool; then peel, seed, and chop. Put the tomatoes in a strainer over a bowl to catch the juice. Reserve separately; you should have about 3 cups pulp and 1 cup juice.

Heat remaining 2 tablespoons extra-virgin olive oil in a large saucepan over medium-high heat until hot. Add garlic and sauté until light brown, moving pan on and off heat as necessary to regulate temperature. Add reserved tomato juice and tomato paste and simmer until thick (tiny bubbles cover the surface). Add tomatoes and continue to simmer until thick but not dry. Season with salt and pepper to taste (it needs a lot of pepper) and add oregano oil. Let cool to room temperature.

Preheat oven to 400 degrees F. Mix together in a bowl bread cubes, oregano olive oil, Parmesan, and salt and pepper to taste. Spread on a cookie sheet or in an oven-going skillet and bake until light brown, about 15 minutes. Immediately remove from oven. Be careful as croutons will continue to darken once removed from oven.

Toss arugula in a bowl with lemon juice, oregano oil, and salt and pepper to taste. Add half the croutons and toss again. Put a large spoonful of soup in each of 4 soup plates and garnish with arugula, remaining croutons, and a sprinkling of Parmesan.

Serves 4.

CHEF'S NOTES: *Grilling the tomatoes brings up their flavor in the same way as adding sun-dried tomatoes to a tomato sauce.*

GARLIC-STUFFED LAMB

If buying fresh lamb, make a double batch and freeze half on the skewers. Convenience and compromise are cousins: Lamb is a meat that freezes very well. Make sure to transfer meat from the freezer to the refrigerator the day before you plan to serve it to ensure even thawing.

1½	pounds (trimmed weight) lamb loin, boned, fat and membranes removed (reserve tenderloins for another use, see Chef's Notes) Oregano Marinade (page 49)
½	cup Roasted Garlic Paste (page 21) Salt and freshly ground pepper
10	large Brussels sprouts, separated into leaves (save innermost leaves and core for another use)
2	tablespoons extra-virgin olive oil
6	ounces fresh wild or shiitake mushrooms, sliced ¼-inch thick
1	tablespoon finely chopped garlic
1	tablespoon finely chopped fresh thyme or 1 teaspoon dried thyme
1	cup lamb stock, chicken stock (page 44) or canned, low-salt chicken broth
3	tablespoons oregano olive oil (page 24)
¼	cup chopped fresh flat-leaf parsley

Slice lamb loin lengthwise (as if filleting) into 2 pieces about ½-inch thick. Using a mallet or the heel of your palm, lightly pound meat to about ¼-inch thickness then cut each in half lengthwise. Place meat in a non-metallic dish and pour marinade over the meat. Turn several times to coat, cover, and refrigerate at least 6 hours or overnight (see Chef's Notes). Turn meat occasionally in marinade.

When ready to cook, prepare grill or preheat broiler. Remove lamb from marinade and discard marinade. Spread about 1 tablespoon garlic paste on each of the lamb pieces. Season with salt and pepper. Roll meat lengthwise end to end and place on skewers. Grill or broil to desired doneness, 10 to 15 minutes for medium-rare meat, depending on heat of grill. Turn meat occasionally to ensure even cooking.

Meanwhile, bring a pot of salted water to a boil. Add Brussels sprout leaves and blanch 10 seconds. Immediately drain and spread on a baking sheet or in a large bowl to cool.

Heat extra-virgin olive oil in a large sauté pan over medium-high heat until almost smoking. Add mushrooms and do not move them for about 1 minute or until lightly brown on one side. Then sauté until brown, about 5 minutes. (It is very important that the mushrooms are not crowded, otherwise they will boil in their own juices rather than brown.)

Add garlic to sauté pan and continue to cook until golden brown, about 1 minute. Add thyme, then Brussels sprout leaves and cook until leaves are wilted and bright green. Add stock and deglaze pan, scraping up all the loose bits on the bottom and edges of the pan. Simmer another 1 to 2 minutes. Add oregano olive oil and parsley. Season to taste with salt and pepper.

To serve, divide mushroom mixture among 4 hot plates and top with lamb. Spoon pan juices over.

Serves 4.

CHEF'S NOTES: *Fresh lamb is typically sold bone in so when you ask your butcher to bone out the loin, you will get the tenderloin as well. If you purchase frozen lamb, usually the loin and tenderloin are sold separately.*

The lamb can marinate as little as 30 minutes if you are in a rush. Brush more marinade on the meat during cooking to add more flavor.

Variation with Sautéed Garlic: If you have not made garlic paste, simply sauté ½ cup finely chopped garlic in 2 tablespoons olive oil until light brown. Spread on the lamb and roll up.

Variation for Mushroom-Stuffed Lamb: You may also spread the sautéed mushrooms (omitting the Brussels sprout leaves) on the lamb and roll up. Make a sauce by reducing the stock by ½ and adding Brussels sprout leaves, oregano oil, and parsley.

OREGANO MARINADE

This is a great marinade for meat and poultry as well as for oily fish such as blue fish, tuna, mackerel, sardines, even swordfish. Lemon zest gives the flavor of lemon without the acidity of juice so you can give fish a lengthy soak. Don't be afraid of twelve hours for thick fillets or whole fish.

½	cup oregano olive oil (page 24)
2	teaspoons finely chopped garlic
½	teaspoon grated lemon zest
¼	teaspoon toasted red pepper flakes (see Chef's Notes) or 1 tablespoon pepper olive oil (page 24)

Put all ingredients in a bowl or jar and mix well. Keeps up to 4 days, refrigerated, in a tightly sealed container.

Makes about ½ cup.

CHEF'S NOTES: *Put red pepper flakes in a skillet and heat over medium heat just until flakes begin to brown. Immediately remove from heat and pour onto a cool dish to prevent burning.*

Rosemary is another Mediterranean herb that often can be interchanged with basil and oregano. It has a strong, pungent, resinous character, which I like but some people may find overwhelming. Infusing it in oil smooths its flavor and allows it to mix easily with other flavors.

I particularly like rosemary for roasting potatoes, with eggplant, and with lamb. It has a particular affinity for fruit including grapes, pears, and oranges. (As an example, I have included a focaccia bread recipe here which includes raisins, fresh grapes, and lemon zest in the dough as well as baked on top. I have never been successful in keeping this bread from being devoured almost as soon as it has been cut into.)

For vegetables with strong flavors of their own, like artichokes and asparagus, rosemary makes a good match. Rosemary also works well with the saltiness of prosciutto as well as with fish with good flavor and meaty texture such as tuna.

ROSEMARY GRILLED AHI WITH ROASTED PEPPER SALAD

I have a five-foot rosemary hedge outside my house from which I can cut long branches for skewers. The rosemary skewers make a dramatic presentation and add flavor; however wooden and metal skewers will work nearly as well.

4	rosemary sprigs (about 6 to 8 inches long) or wood or metal skewers
4	center-cut ahi tuna steaks (about 5 ounces each), cut into blocks ¾ to 1 inch thick and 3 inches long
¼	cup Rosemary and Roasted Lemon Marinade (page 59)
	Salt and freshly ground pepper
3	cups Roasted Pepper Salad
4	cups green salad (optional), lightly dressed with Balsamic Basil Vinaigrette (page 29)

Soak rosemary or wooden skewers in water to cover 1 to 2 hours. Preheat grill or broiler. Skewer 2 tuna pieces lengthwise on each rosemary sprig and brush with marinade. Season with salt and pepper and grill, turning once or twice, to medium rare, 8 to 10 minutes, depending on heat.

Place a tuna skewer on each plate and top with ¾ cup Roasted Pepper Salad; make sure to spoon some juices from the salad over each serving. Garnish with green salad, if you like. Serve immediately.

Serves 4.

ROASTED PEPPER SALAD— PEPPERONATA

I grew up on pepperonata served as a side dish with spiced flank steak. This is a very versatile salad: Serve it as a side vegetable, put it on pizza or in a crusty roll with arugula and slices of Italian cured meats. If you like spicy food, add a pinch of toasted, ground chili peppers.

12	large red and yellow bell peppers (about 5 pounds)
½	cup peeled, seeded, and chopped vine-ripened, red tomatoes or good-quality canned, plum (Roma) tomatoes
1	tablespoon finely chopped garlic
¼	cup rinsed, drained, and roughly chopped capers
¼	cup finely chopped fresh flat-leaf parsley
2	tablespoons rosemary olive oil (page 24)
6	tablespoons extra-virgin olive oil
3	tablespoons champagne wine vinegar or white wine vinegar
¼	cup pitted ripe olives (such as Kalamata)
	Salt and freshly ground pepper

Preheat broiler. Roast the peppers in the broiler or over an open flame or grill until skins are charred all over. Place in a plastic bag and close to steam the skins loose or use a bowl and lid. When cool, peel off the charred skins. Remove and discard core, seeds, and veins; reserve their juices. Cut the peppers into strips about ½-inch wide.

Place peppers and their juices in a mixing bowl and combine with the remaining ingredients. Adjust seasoning with salt and pepper. Let rest 30 minutes before serving. Salad keeps up to 4 days, refrigerated, in a tightly sealed container.

Makes about 6 cups.

CHEF'S NOTES: *Roasted garlic olive oil may be substituted for rosemary olive oil or use a tablespoon of each.*

HARVEST FOCACCIA

In Tuscany, this bread was traditionally made on the first day of harvest as a snack for the field workers with this year's grapes and the raisins of the previous harvest. Serve it for breakfast, as a spuntino (midday snack), as part of an antipasto with prosciutto, or with cheeses as a cheese course. The recipe makes a soft, tender, and delicious bread blending sweet and savory flavors. The recipe may be doubled if your mixer will hold ten cups of flour.

1	ounce fresh yeast or 2 envelopes active dry yeast
2	cups lukewarm whole milk
1	tablespoon plus 1 teaspoon sugar
5	cups all-purpose flour plus more for sprinkling the work surface
1/3	(about) cup rosemary olive oil (page 24)
1	tablespoon finely chopped fresh rosemary (optional)
1	tablespoon grated lemon zest
1	cup halved or quartered red grapes
1	cup golden raisins
1½	teaspoons salt
1	whole egg, beaten with a fork until frothy Coarse salt

In a large bowl or the work bowl of an electric mixer, dissolve yeast in lukewarm milk and add 1 tablespoon sugar and 1 cup of the flour. Mix well and let stand in a warm place about 15 minutes for the yeast to activate.

In a small saucepan, warm ¼ cup of the rosemary oil with chopped rosemary and lemon zest. Add grapes and raisins, mix well, and add ½ to yeast mixture. Mix another 1 cup flour into yeast mixture with the dough hook attachment. Knead until smooth. With machine running, add salt and remaining 3 cups flour, 1 cup at a time, kneading until smooth after each addition. Knead another 6 minutes after final addition of flour. The dough

should remain rather wet to ensure a soft and light bread. Shape dough into a ball on a floured board and put in an oiled bowl. Cover with a damp towel and allow to rise in a warm place until doubled in bulk, about 45 minutes.

Punch dough down and lightly sprinkle work surface with flour. Turn out dough and knead lightly. At this point, dough may be wrapped and frozen.

If ready to bake, preheat oven to 400 degrees F. Oil a baking sheet. Press dough down into a flat disc with the heel of your hand. (Dough is pliable and easy to work.) Using your fingertips, nudge the dough into a rectangle. Stretch and pull the dough and nudge it into shape to fit a cookie sheet. Dough can be rolled but the pressure will produce a heavier bread; the irregularities of hand shaping are part of the bread's charm. Transfer dough to oiled baking sheet and brush with 2 tablespoons rosemary oil. Let rise again in a warm place until doubled, 30 to 40 minutes.

Make indentations all over the dough by pressing with your fingertips being careful not to puncture all the way through the dough. Bake 15 minutes, remove from oven, and brush with beaten egg. Sprinkle with remaining 1 teaspoon sugar and spread with remaining rosemary oil-grape mixture and a light sprinkling of coarse salt. Return to oven and continue to bake until golden brown on top and crisp on the bottom, about 10 minutes. Let cool in pan to room temperature before cutting.

Makes 3 pounds dough; enough for 1 standard, 11 x 17-inch baking sheet.

CHEF'S NOTES: *Dough may also be cut and shaped into three 1-pound pieces. Each piece can be shaped into a 10-inch round.*

Variation for Bread Sticks: The same dough may be used to make bread sticks. Cut off 2-ounce portions of dough and roll under the palms of your hands into long rolls. Their irregularities are part of their charm. Brush with flavored or plain olive oil and roll in seeds such as poppy, sesame, or fennel or a mixture of all, if desired. Transfer to an oiled cookie sheet and let rise in a warm place until doubled in bulk, about 15 minutes. Bake in a preheated 400 degree F oven until golden brown, about 15 minutes.

PASTA WITH ROASTED EGGPLANT SAUCE

This is a very quick, simple, homey pasta. It is very Italian in that the sauce coats the pasta without a pool of extra sauce. It may not be very colorful, but it tastes great.

½	cup chicken stock (page 44) or canned low-salt chicken broth
1½	cups Rosemary–Roasted Eggplant Paste Salt and freshly ground pepper
1	pound dried pasta (shape of your choice)
3	cups loosely packed arugula or baby spinach, roughly chopped if leaves are large
¼	cup finely chopped fresh flat-leaf parsley
1	cup freshly grated Parmesan cheese

In a medium saucepan, bring stock to a boil over medium-high heat. Lower heat to medium and whisk in eggplant paste. Adjust seasoning with salt and pepper to taste.

Meanwhile, cook pasta until al dente in lots of boiling, salted water. When cooked, drain well, reserving ½ cup of the cooking liquid, and immediately return pasta to the cooking pot. Add arugula to pasta and toss so arugula begins to heat and wilt. Add eggplant mixture and parsley and mix well. Add some of the reserved pasta cooking liquid if sauce seems too thick.

Pour onto a heated platter or serving bowl or divide among 4 to 6 hot bowls. Sprinkle with Parmesan and serve.

Serves 4 to 6.

ROSEMARY–ROASTED EGGPLANT PASTE

This simple dish makes a great appetizer spread on bread, a sauce for a tomatoless pizza, or a dip for vegetables. It also makes a delicious, easy pasta sauce when thinned with vegetable or chicken stock (page 44). The blacker the eggplant gets during roasting, the smokier the flavor becomes.

1	large eggplant (about 1½ pounds)
4	tablespoons extra-virgin olive oil
½	tablespoon rosemary olive oil (page 24)
½	tablespoon roasted garlic oil or 2 tablespoons Roasted Garlic Paste (page 21) Salt and freshly ground pepper

Preheat broiler and set rack to low. Use your hands to lightly oil eggplant with 1 tablespoon of the extra-virgin olive oil and place on a baking sheet. Roast, turning occasionally, until very soft and black, about 45 minutes. Set aside to cool.

Scrape eggplant pulp into the work bowl of a food processor. If seeds are large, cut out and discard. Process until smooth. Add flavored oils and remaining 3 tablespoons extra-virgin olive oil and process again. Season with salt and pepper to taste. Keeps up to 4 days refrigerated in a tightly sealed container.

Makes 1 to 1½ cups.

CHEF'S NOTES: *Try grilling the eggplant on a summer evening after you have finishing barbecuing supper. Just put the whole, oiled eggplant on the grill and cover with the lid. Turn occasionally until very soft. Finish cooking in the oven if the fire burns down before the eggplant is sufficiently black and soft. The smokiness of the grill will add another flavor dimension to the purée.*

SHAVED ARTICHOKE
AND ASPARAGUS SALAD

This spring I was inspired by the beautiful artichokes in the markets to create a new, raw artichoke salad. It can be turned into a main dish salad with the addition of a piece of sautéed or roasted fish such as halibut.

8	medium-sized artichokes
½	cup fresh lemon juice (preferably from Meyer lemons)
18	spears asparagus, trimmed and ends peeled
¼	cup rosemary olive oil (page 24)
1	cup extra-virgin olive oil
2	tablespoons chopped fresh flat-leaf parsley
	Salt and freshly ground pepper
2	ounces Parmesan or pecorino cheese

Bring a large pot of salted water to a boil. Cut off and discard the top third of the artichokes. Snap off the dark, outer leaves until only the pale, yellow-green leaves remain. Cut off all but 1 inch of the stem. With a paring knife, trim artichokes and their stems of all remaining dark green parts. Cut in half lengthwise through the hearts and remove fuzzy chokes with a spoon. Slice halves lengthwise very thinly and put in a bowl of water with 2 tablespoons of the lemon juice.

When the salted water boils, add asparagus and blanch until just tender, about 5 minutes. Immediately drain and plunge into a bowl of ice water. Drain again. Drain artichokes well and put in a bowl with the remaining lemon juice, olive oils, and parsley. Season with salt and pepper. Toss well. Moisten asparagus with some of the dressing.

To serve, mound a portion of artichoke salad on each of 6 plates and top each with 3 asparagus spears. With a vegetable peeler, shave strips of Parmesan or pecorino over the top and serve.

Serves 6.

Variation with Grilled Asparagus: Blanch asparagus 2 to 3 minutes or until slightly undercooked. Brush with a tablespoon rosemary oil and grill until tender, turning occasionally to ensure even cooking, 2 to 3 minutes.

SPRING VEGETABLE RICE SALAD WITH ROSEMARY-LEMON VINAIGRETTE

This is really a vegetable salad with rice. Feel free to substitute any of your favorite vegetables or whatever is abundant in your garden such as tomatoes, eggplant, bell peppers, and green beans.

1	pound fresh fava beans, black-eyed peas, or lima beans
1	pound fresh peas (about 10 ounces shelled)
1	zucchini (½ pound), cut into ¼-inch dice
2	ears corn, kernels cut off the cob
¼	pound prosciutto, cut into paper thin slices
1	teaspoon grated lemon zest
3	cups cooked long-grain white rice
¼	cup rosemary olive oil (page 24)
¼	cup extra-virgin olive oil
¼	cup fresh lemon juice
2	tablespoons chopped fresh flat-leaf parsley
1	small, red onion, cut into ¼-inch dice
	Salt and freshly ground pepper

Bring a large pot of salted water to a boil. Blanch the vegetables, one at a time, until they are just tender. As they are cooked, drain and spread them out on a cookie sheet to cool (see Chef's Notes). When cool, peel fava beans and mix with other vegetables in a serving bowl. Cut half of the prosciutto into julienne and add it to the vegetables with the lemon zest and rice. Toss well.

For the dressing, mix together in a bowl or jar the rosemary and extra-virgin olive oils, lemon juice, parsley, red onion, and salt and pepper to taste. Let sit at least 10 minutes before mixing with the salad.

When ready to serve, whisk dressing well again; then pour over the salad and toss well. Adjust seasoning. Arrange salad on 6 chilled plates. Lay 2 slices prosciutto over half of each salad and serve.

Serves 6.

CHEF'S NOTES: *I do not use an ice bath to stop further cooking of blanched vegetables unless I have to (for instance, for asparagus) but prefer to "pan shock" vegetables: spreading them on a baking sheet to cool. To preserve vitamins and minerals, you might want to cook the rice in the vegetable cooking water. Just remember to measure the water to make sure there is enough to cook the rice. Add more boiling water if necessary.*

ROSEMARY MARINADE

Rosemary marinade is delicious brushed on meat and poultry such as lamb, chicken, turkey and veal before and during cooking. It gives a wonderful flavor to grilled vegetables such as radicchio, peppers, eggplant, and zucchini. The marinade may also be simply drizzled over a finished dish as a sauce.

10	oil-packed anchovy fillets, well drained and minced
2	teaspoons finely chopped garlic
2	teaspoons capers, rinsed, drained, and chopped if large
¼	cup red wine vinegar
½	cup rosemary olive oil (page 24)
½	cup extra-virgin olive oil
2	teaspoons finely chopped fresh flat-leaf parsley
	Freshly ground pepper to taste

Combine anchovy fillets, garlic, and capers in a mixing bowl. Mix well. Whisk in red wine vinegar. Slowly add rosemary oil and extra-virgin olive oil, while whisking, to form an emulsion. Add parsley and pepper to taste. (The marinade may also be made in a blender or food processor.) Keeps up to 1 week refrigerated in a tightly sealed container.

Makes about 1 cup.

Variation with Grilled Radicchio: Cut each whole radicchio head into 4 wedges. Lightly coat with marinade and grill over medium heat until tender. Drizzle with more marinade before serving. Serve as a side dish.

ROSEMARY AND ROASTED LEMON MARINADE

By roasting the lemons, their acidity mellows considerably. We often use this technique when creating wine dinners so the food will not conflict with the wines.

6	lemons, cut in half
	Salt and freshly ground pepper
2	teaspoons finely chopped garlic
⅔	cup rosemary olive oil (page 24)
⅓	cup extra-virgin olive oil

Preheat broiler. Place lemons, cut side up, in a small, nonaluminum baking dish and sprinkle with salt and pepper. Roast, about 6 inches below the heat, until very soft, about 20 minutes. The tops will darken and caramelize. Let cool in the baking dish.

Squeeze the lemon pulp and juice and scrape all the cooking juices from the baking dish into a strainer supported over a bowl. Force it through and add garlic. Whisk in rosemary oil and extra-virgin olive oil. Keeps up to 1 week refrigerated in a tightly sealed container.

To marinate: Lightly coat chicken pieces or whole birds with marinade, cover with plastic wrap, and let stand, refrigerated, 24 hours. Marinate fish for 12 hours.

Makes about 1½ cups.

ROASTed GARLic
Olive Oil

Roasted garlic olive oil is the second oil I made after basil; it and the basil oil are still the most popular flavors. We use a great deal of garlic at Tra Vigne, sautéing it until pale gold or roasting whole heads to make a paste. Using roasted garlic oil means you can achieve the same flavor without the fuss and mess!

While I prefer the taste of cooked garlic to raw, a garlic oil flavored with raw garlic can be readily substituted in any of the recipes. A spoonful or two of roasted garlic paste will also achieve a similar effect as the oil. Because the garlic in roasted garlic oil is already a cooked, caramelized flavor, you can sauté in roasted garlic oil without much loss of the garlicky flavor. The taste of a raw garlic oil will change if subjected to heat.

Roasted garlic oil is one of the most versatile flavored olive oils. Use it to sauté vegetables such as sliced asparagus. Topped with a few toasted, chopped almonds, you will have created a dish fit for company or even, with a piece of Parmesan cheese and bread, a weeknight supper.

Use roasted garlic oil as a base to flavor grains and pasta dishes. In fact, it can be a pasta sauce on its own with the addition of chopped parsley, grated cheese, and salt and pepper.

SAUTÉED SPINACH

Roasted garlic oil does wonderful things for vegetables so easily! A simple vegetable dish becomes suddenly exciting. Try sautéing English and sugar snap peas, asparagus cut in rounds on the diagonal, arugula, kale, even red bell peppers.

- 4 slices bacon, diced
- ¼ cup roasted garlic olive oil (page 21)
- 2 bunches fresh spinach, washed and dried
  Salt and freshly ground pepper

In a large sauté pan, slowly cook bacon until crisp. Remove bacon and drain on paper towel. Pour off fat from the pan and add garlic oil. Heat over medium-high heat. Add spinach and sauté quickly until wilted and dry. Season with salt and pepper and serve.

Serves 4 as a side dish.

Variation with Pasta: For a light, quick entrée, toss the spinach with ½ pound pasta, cooked al dente, and ¼ to ½ cup freshly grated Parmesan cheese.

WARM SHRIMP AND ARUGULA SALAD

This adaptation of a slow, oven method for cooking fish was taught to me by Lydia Bastianich of Felidia Restaurant in Manhattan. It gives very tender results, especially important if you are using frozen shrimp! Here, I use it for shrimp but I also use it for oysters, clams, scallops, and squid. While the recipe can be completed on top of the stove, I find it easier to put the fish in the oven as described here; this frees the cook for several minutes for other tasks.

- 6 tablespoons roasted garlic olive oil (page 21)
- 1⅓ pounds large shrimp with shells,
  peeled and deveined
  Salt and freshly ground pepper
- ½ cup dry white wine
- 1 tablespoon fresh lemon juice
- 1 large vine-ripened tomato,
  peeled, seeded, and chopped
- ¼ cup finely chopped fresh flat-leaf parsley
- 2 bunches arugula

Preheat oven to 300 degrees F. Heat 3 tablespoons of the garlic oil in a large, oven-going sauté pan until very hot over medium heat. Season shrimp with salt and pepper and add to pan. Cook over low heat for a few seconds, just until shrimp begin to give up their juices. Add white wine and immediately put pan in preheated oven 2 to 4 minutes or until fish is just cooked. Do not overcook!

Remove shrimp to a bowl with a slotted spoon. Add lemon juice to cooking liquids in sauté pan and boil rapidly until reduced by half. Remove pan from heat and immediately add remaining 3 tablespoons oil, tomato, parsley, arugula, and shrimp. Toss well. Shrimp should be just barely warm and arugula barely wilted.

Serves 4 as an entrée; 6 to 8 as an appetizer.

ROASTED GARLIC
CAESAR SALAD

Caesar salad dressing may also be used as a dip for vegetables or as a spread for sandwiches such as roasted or grilled vegetables and chicken. Depending on how richly you like your salad dressed, use about three-fourths of the dressing for the salad and keep the rest on hand. Or forget salad entirely and use the dressing to sauce baked potatoes instead! If you are concerned about using raw eggs, see variation at end of recipe.

8	anchovy fillets, drained well
1	tablespoon Dijon mustard
2	tablespoons fresh lemon juice
1	tablespoon champagne wine vinegar or white wine vinegar
	Freshly ground pepper
1	egg yolk
	Dash Worcestershire sauce
1¼	cups roasted garlic olive oil (page 21)
1	cup freshly grated Parmesan cheese
2-3	heads romaine lettuce
	Garlic croutons (see Chef's Notes)

Combine anchovies, mustard, lemon juice, vinegar, pepper, egg yolk, and Worcestershire sauce in a blender or food processor. Blend until smooth. With machine running, slowly add roasted garlic oil to form an emulsion. Thin, if necessary, with warm water. Add ½ cup Parmesan and mix in with a few brief pulses. Adjust seasoning. Sauce can be made up to 2 days ahead. Refrigerate in a tightly covered container.

To make the salad, remove outer leaves of romaine until remaining are firm and pale green. Separate into leaves and put into a salad bowl. Pour about ¾ths of the dressing over the lettuce, add garlic croutons, and toss well. Pass the remaining Parmesan at table.

Serves 3 to 4; makes about 1¼ cups dressing.

Variation with Pasteurized Liquid Eggs and Cholesterol-Free Liquid Eggs: Follow directions on the package and use the equivalent of 1 whole egg for the mayonnaise recipes in this book. Cholesterol-free liquid eggs, such as Egg Beaters, are readily available and work for these recipes as well. Use ¼ cup liquid egg and 1 tablespoon vinegar or lemon juice and proceed with the recipe as written. The texture is very light but the emulsion does not break and it tastes very good. There is the added benefit of enjoying mayonnaise without fear of cholesterol!

CHEF'S NOTES: *Easy croutons: Preheat oven to 350 degrees F. Cut four ½-inch thick slices of country bread (including crusts) into small cubes. Toss with 1 tablespoon garlic oil and season with salt and pepper. Bake about 10 minutes or until toasted with a little softness left in the center.*

GRILLED STEAK WITH GARLIC SMASHED POTATOES

I gave some flavored oils to Mike Moone when we were considering our joint venture, Napa Valley Kitchens, producers of specialty foods. He used them that night on a barbecued steak and called me the next morning to seal our deal. This is an adaptation of his recipe. The combination of porcini and garlic oil gives a deep, sweet, earthy flavor, soylike without the saltiness.

2	pounds flank steak (or other preferred cut such as London Broil)
	Roasted Garlic and Porcini Marinade
	Salt and freshly ground pepper
2	tablespoons roasted garlic olive oil (page 21)
3	tablespoons porcini olive oil (page 24)
	Garlic Smashed Potatoes (page 67)

Flank steak tends to curl on a barbecue. To prevent this, prick the steak all over with the point of a knife. This will tenderize the meat, allow the marinade to penetrate more readily, and prevent the meat from curling on the grill.

Pour marinade over the steak in a nonaluminum dish. Turn meat several times to coat evenly with marinade. Cover and refrigerate 2 hours or overnight (see Chef's Notes). Turn occasionally.

When ready to cook, preheat grill or broiler. Season steak with salt and pepper on both sides and grill or broil to desired doneness, 7 to 10 minutes for medium rare, depending on heat of the grill. When done, remove meat to a heated platter and drizzle the garlic and porcini oils over the steak. Let rest 5 to 6 minutes. Slice steak thinly reserving juices in the platter. To serve, place the sliced meat over the hot smashed potatoes and pour the juices over all.

Serves 4.

CHEF'S NOTES: *Remember to oil your grill well to prevent sticking or invest in a nonstick or cast iron insert.*

The steak can be cooked immediately upon being coated with marinade if you are rushed. There will be a little less flavor than if given a longer time to marinate.

ROASTED GARLIC AND PORCINI MARINADE

This has a robust flavor, great for meats with lots of flavor such as beef, lamb, and pork. Use for a crown roast of pork or simply brush on one side of a steak, grill, turn and brush the second side.

2	teaspoons Dijon mustard
2	tablespoons roasted garlic olive oil (page 21)
2	tablespoons porcini olive oil (page 24)
½	teaspoon chopped fresh thyme or pinch dried thyme
½	teaspoon chopped fresh oregano or pinch dried oregano
1½	tablespoons fresh lemon juice
½	teaspoon red pepper flakes
½	teaspoon freshly ground pepper

Place marinade ingredients in a blender or food processor and blend until smooth. Brush on meats before cooking; baste occasionally during cooking with more marinade.

Makes about ½ cup.

GARLIC SMASHED POTATOES

This is it — the mashed potato recipe you will use for the rest of your culinary life! I occasionally use the same recipe for sweet potatoes. Make more potatoes than you think you need. They will all disappear!

2	pounds baking potatoes, peeled and cut into large chunks
1	tablespoon unsalted butter
½	cup heavy cream
½	cup roasted garlic olive oil (page 21)
	Salt and freshly ground pepper
2	tablespoons chopped fresh chives

Cook potatoes in a large pot of boiling, salted water until fork tender. Drain well and let dry on a baking pan 5 minutes.

In a large bowl, begin mashing the potatoes with the butter using an electric mixer. Heat cream to a boil, add to potatoes, and continue to beat. Add garlic oil and beat again. Season with salt and pepper to taste. Beat in chives. If too thick, thin with warm milk. Reheat, if necessary (this is most easily done in a microwave oven).

Serves 4.

CHEF'S NOTES: *If you love garlic, the potatoes will easily absorb more garlic oil, up to another ½ cup. The result is a luxuriously smooth purée redolent of roast garlic.*

Variation with Other Vegetables: Feel free to add other vegetable purées to the potatoes such as asparagus or roasted peppers. Depending on the moistness of the added vegetable purée, you can use up to equal proportions of each. If the result is too wet, simply stir it over heat in a pot until it reaches its desired consistency.

SPAGHETTINI WITH ROASTED GARLIC OIL

Without a doubt, this is my favorite late-night pasta. Not only is it easy to digest, it is very quickly cooked and even easier to clean up!

1	pound dried spaghettini
¾	cup roasted garlic olive oil (page 21)
½	teaspoon chili flakes
½	cup chicken stock (page 44) or canned, low-salt chicken broth or pasta cooking liquid
	Salt and freshly ground pepper
1	cup freshly grated Parmesan cheese
3	tablespoons finely chopped fresh flat-leaf parsley

Bring a large pot of salted water to a vigorous boil and add pasta a handful at a time so water stays at a boil. Cook until al dente, 7 to 8 minutes.

While pasta is cooking, warm ¼ cup of the roasted garlic oil with the chili flakes in a large saucepan over medium heat. Heat just until chili flakes begin to move and sizzle.

When pasta is done, drain well and toss in the saucepan with the oil and chili flakes. Add stock and season with salt and pepper. Add remaining ½ cup oil, ¾ cup of the cheese, and the parsley and toss again. Serve immediately in warmed bowls, topped with remaining cheese.

Serves 4 to 6.

There are many pepper and chili oils on the market. Some have dried chilies in the bottle; some have a blend of chilies, black pepper, and herbs. Each will have its own flavor and degree of heat. With the exception of Chinese chili oils, which are fiery hot, any of the pepper oils will work with these recipes. However, I recommend you taste your oil — commercial or homemade — to determine its heat before starting a preparation, then adjusting the amount you use.

Pepper oils may be used for sautéing and roasting without great loss of flavor; however, the subtleties of flavor in fresh, uncooked chilies or bell peppers may be lost with high heat cooking. Eggs — from simple fried eggs to omelets — are terrific cooked in pepper oil. Seafood, too, including shrimp and scallops, are delicious cooked with pepper oil. Pepper oil is a natural for any dish with a Southwestern bent. And try popcorn with pepper oil!

SCRAMBLED EGGS WITH PEPPER OIL

Eggs scrambled slowly over low heat are always welcome for a leisurely breakfast. When the eggs are scrambled in pepper oil, then the taste is both comforting and invigorating! Make them for supper and serve with a simple green salad.

4	tablespoons pepper olive oil (page 24)
1	tablespoon finely chopped garlic
4	slices crusty Italian bread
8	eggs
2	tablespoons cream or milk
½	tablespoon chopped fresh oregano or 1 teaspoon dried oregano
	Salt and freshly ground pepper

Heat 2 tablespoons of the pepper oil in a nonstick skillet over medium heat. Add garlic and cook gently until transparent, about 3 minutes. Let cool a minute or two, then brush garlic and oil on one side of the bread. Toast or grill bread and keep warm.

Heat remaining 2 tablespoons oil in the same pan over medium-low heat. Break eggs into a mixing bowl, add cream or milk, and oregano, and season with salt and pepper. Mix well with a fork or whisk. Pour into the heated pan and cook slowly folding the eggs over themselves until cooked to desired degree. Put a garlic toast on each of 4 plates and spoon eggs over.

Serves 4.

GRILLED CHICKEN SALAD SANDWICH

The color of the pepper aioli turns the salad a pretty salmon pink color. The proportions make a crunchy salad; if you prefer more meat to vegetables, add another chicken breast.

1	whole, large chicken breast, boned, skin on
	Salt and freshly ground pepper
¼	cup finely chopped onion
2	tablespoons finely chopped carrot
2	tablespoons finely chopped celery
1	tablespoon finely chopped fresh flat-leaf parsley
1	tablespoon finely chopped fresh oregano
¾	cup Pepper Aioli (page 74)
1	tablespoon milk or buttermilk (optional)
8	slices toasted or grilled crusty Italian bread
	Crisp lettuce (such as iceberg, butter or bibb)

Preheat grill or broiler. Season chicken on both sides with salt and pepper and grill until done, about 7 minutes. Let cool. Discard skin and cut meat into large dice. Put in a mixing bowl.

Add onion, carrot, celery, parsley, and oregano. Mix in pepper aioli. Season with salt and pepper to taste. If salad is too thick, thin with milk or buttermilk. Spread a little of the salad on each slice of bread. Top 4 slices with lettuce, top with 2nd slice and press down. Slice in half diagonally.

Makes 4 sandwiches.

SWORDFISH WITH MEDITERRANEAN TOMATO SAUCE AND LINGUINI

This recipe is an adaptation of a fresh Mediterranean tomato sauce from Carol Dearth who currently lives in the Pacific Northwest. She created the recipe for a contest for my Consorzio flavored olive oils. Carol, who lived in Naples for two years, credits the Italians with teaching her the importance of using very, very fresh ingredients and treating them simply and intelligently. The recipe makes more tomato sauce than you will need for the fish. It is delicious as a pasta sauce, a topping for bruschetta, or a sauce or side dish for grilled poultry or meat. For the best flavor, use garden fresh tomatoes.

3	cups vine-ripened plum (Roma) tomatoes, cored and cut into thin wedges
	Salt and freshly ground pepper
1	tablespoon finely chopped fresh oregano or 1 teaspoon dried oregano
1	tablespoon finely chopped fresh flat-leaf parsley
1	tablespoon minced garlic
¼	cup minced red onion
2	tablespoons rinsed, drained, and roughly chopped capers
½	cup roasted, seeded, and coarsely chopped red or yellow bell pepper (page 93)
12	pitted and sliced Greek olives (such as Kalamata or Gaeta olives)
2	tablespoons fresh lemon juice
2	tablespoons pepper olive oil (page 24)
6	tablespoons extra-virgin olive oil
½	pound dried linguini
4	large sheets parchment paper or waxed paper (see Chef's Notes)
4	swordfish steaks (5 ounces each)

Put tomatoes in a large bowl and season with salt and pepper to taste. Add oregano, parsley, garlic, onion, capers, peppers, olives, lemon juice, pepper oil, and 4 tablespoons of the extra-virgin olive oil. Stir gently just to mix and set aside at least 1 hour. Adjust seasonings if desired. Mixture will become more liquid and saucelike over time.

Preheat oven to 450 degrees F. Bring a large pot of salted water to a boil and cook linguini until al dente. Drain and toss with remaining 2 tablespoons extra-virgin olive oil. Reserve.

Fold 4 large sheets of parchment paper in half. With the fold as the spine, cut a large semicircle (about an 8-inch radius) with one end more pointed than the other (opened out, the shape resembles a heart). Open the circles and arrange a small pile of linguini in the center of one side of each of the 4 sheets. Top with a spoonful of tomato sauce, making sure to moisten the linguini with the juices. Lay a piece of fish on top and arrange with another spoonful of sauce. Moisten again with juices from the sauce and season with salt and pepper. Leave a 1-inch border of paper clear.

Close the parchment over the fish. Starting at the flatter end of the semicircle, firmly fold the edge inwards. Fold entire edge into a series of tight, flat, overlapping "pleats" to enclose the fish. Fold the last pleat several times and tuck it under the "bag."
Put the "bags" on a baking sheet and bake in the oven 12 to 15 minutes. The bags will puff up and brown. To serve, transfer the bags to 4 warmed dinner plates and let each diner cut open the package to enjoy the aromas.

Serves 4; makes about 1 quart sauce.

CHEF'S NOTES: *Waxed paper is a nice touch to make the cooking "bags" because you can see the colors of the sauce through it.*

BRODETTO OF MANILA CLAMS AND DRIED SAUSAGE

This brodetto (seafood broth) is a typical southern Italian fisher-man's lunch. He would take along with him bread, dried sausage, and white or red wine. The seafood he would add from his catch. I like to use a baguette studded with olives but a plain baguette will do very well. This recipe is also delicious as a pasta sauce.

1½	pounds medium-sized manila clams in shells
2	tablespoons butter
4	pieces baguette (each 2 to 3 inches long)
3	tablespoons pepper olive oil (page 24)
2	tablespoons thinly sliced garlic
1	cup dry white wine
⅓	pound spicy, dry sausage, cut into ⅓-inch dice
	Salt and freshly ground pepper
¼	cup finely chopped fresh flat-leaf parsley

Scrub clams very well in fresh water. Discard any that are open and do not close when poked. Let soak in cold water until ready to use.

Preheat oven to 425 degrees F. Heat butter over medium heat in a large, oven-going sauté pan until butter turns a light brown. Add baguette pieces and toss to coat all over with butter. Put in oven and bake until crust is brown and well developed, about 10 minutes. Turn, if necessary, to brown evenly all over. Drain on paper towels and keep warm.

Heat pepper oil in a sauté pan over medium-high heat until hot. Add garlic and sauté until garlic is lightly brown, 10 to 15 seconds. Regulate heat by moving the pan on and off the heat.

Add clams to sauté pan and stir well. Add white wine, turn heat to high, and cook, stirring the clams occasionally, until they have popped open, about 5 minutes. Add sausage halfway through the cooking. Discard any clams that remain closed. Simmer rapidly until liquid has reduced by half. Season with salt and pepper. Add chopped parsley and mix well. Put one toasted baguette piece, cut side up, in each soup plate and pour clam mixture over.

Serve immediately. Serves 4.

Variation with Mussels: You can use mussels instead of clams and spicy Italian sausage (just remember to cook and drain the sausage first).

PEPPER AIOLI

The bread crumbs give the sauce a completely different texture: less oily, lighter. They also prevent the sauce from separating when adding it to hot soups, for instance. Use this aioli as a sandwich spread, to enrich a fish soup, to perk up a grilled chicken breast, and to spoon over a broiled steak. It is also delicious with any kind of shellfish. If you are concerned about using raw eggs, see variation at end of recipe.

2	garlic cloves, finely chopped
1	egg yolk
1	tablespoon fresh lemon juice
¾	cup pepper olive oil (page 24) or half pepper olive oil and half olive oil
	Salt and freshly ground pepper
¼	cup fine, dried white bread crumbs

Put garlic, egg yolk, and lemon juice in a food processor or blender and process. With machine running, add pepper oil drop by drop until an emulsion forms, then pour in a slow steady stream. Thin, if necessary, with a tablespoon warm water. Season to taste with salt and pepper and pulse in bread crumbs.

Makes about 1 cup.

Citrus Oil Variation: Make the sauce with citrus oil instead of pepper oil and serve with Marinated Grilled Shrimp Cocktail, page 88.

Variation with Pasteurized Liquid Eggs and Cholesterol-Free Liquid Eggs: Follow directions on the package and use the equivalent of 1 whole egg for the mayonnaise recipes in this book. Cholesterol-free liquid eggs, such as Egg Beaters, are readily available and work for these recipes as well. Use ¼ cup liquid egg and 1 tablespoon vinegar or lemon juice and proceed with the recipe as written. The texture is very light but the emulsion does not break and it tastes very good. There is the added benefit of enjoying mayonnaise without fear of cholesterol!

PASTINA RISOTTO
WITH ROASTED PEPPERS
AND BROCCOLI

This dish was inspired by Nick Morfogen. He was my executive sous-chef at Tra Vigne until 1993 when we opened Ajax Mountain Tavern in Aspen, Colorado, and made him chef and partner in the new venture. Pastina is the most comforting of all pastas for Italians to eat because it is the pasta of childhood. Pastina is the diminutive form of the word pasta. *And pastina is exactly that — tiny little grains of pasta that look more like a cooked grain than a pasta. This dish can be varied according to the season by adding whatever vegetables are best: Peas and asparagus are two of my favorites.*

1	pound dried pastina (#78 *Acini di Pepe*)
5	tablespoons pepper olive oil (page 24)
2	tablespoons chopped garlic
3	cups broccoli florets
	Salt and freshly ground pepper
2	tablespoons chopped fresh thyme
3	cups hot chicken stock (page 44) or canned, low-salt chicken broth or vegetable broth
3	red bell peppers, roasted, peeled, seeded, and cut into ½-inch dice (page 93)
1	cup freshly grated Parmesan cheese
½	stick (4 tablespoons) butter (optional)

Bring a large pot of salted water to a boil. Add pastina and cook until it is slightly undercooked, about 11 minutes. Make sure to stir occasionally during cooking or the pasta will stick to the bottom of the pan. Drain pasta and run under cold water to stop the cooking. Drain again and reserve.

Heat oil in a saucepan over medium-high heat until hot. Add garlic and cook until light brown, moving pan on and off heat as necessary to regulate temperature. Add broccoli and cook until it turns bright green, about 1 minute. Season with salt and pepper. Add thyme; it should make a crackling sound as it hits the hot pan.

Add stock to broccoli mixture and bring to a boil over high heat. Boil until reduced by half. Add peppers and cooked pastina and return mixture to a boil. Stir in ¾ cup of the Parmesan and season with salt and pepper. Swirl in butter, if desired, for a richer-tasting dish. Pour into a heated serving bowl or individual soup plates and sprinkle with remaining ¼ cup cheese.

Serves 6.

CHEF'S NOTES: *The preparation of this dish resembles that for risotto, thus the name, but it takes less time and can be prepared ahead of time without loss of quality. Follow the recipe through the reduction of the stock. Reserve the pasta and broth separately then assemble the dish in minutes when ready to serve.*

PORCINI

Olive Oil

Fresh, wild mushrooms, especially porcini, can often run up to twenty-five dollars a pound when you can find them. Shiitakes are being grown commercially and so are more available and less expensive but still cost an average of twelve to fifteen dollars per pound. By using a mushroom infused oil such as porcini olive oil combined with domestic mushrooms in a dish calling for wild mushrooms, you can achieve much of the same flavor as wild mushrooms more economically.

One of the great pleasures of cooking occurs when an experiment turns out far better than you expected. Such is the case with cooking with porcini oil. It takes on a sweet, earthy flavor which took me completely by surprise. This oil can add a meaty flavor to vegetarian dishes, one of the hardest things to do. Porcini oil is also a wonderful complementary flavor with pancetta and pork as well as dried fruits. Porcini oil works with any food you might imagine good with mushrooms such as beef and lamb.

WARM GOAT CHEESE
AND PANCETTA SALAD

MUSHROOM HASH

OVEN-ROASTED
VEGETABLES

MUSHROOM AND
ARTICHOKE
PAPPARDELLE

PORK TENDERLOIN
WITH MOLASSES, BACON,
AND PORCINI
VINAIGRETTE

WARM GOAT CHEESE AND PANCETTA SALAD

I created this recipe for my friend, goat cheese maker Laura Chenel, about five years ago. It has been on Tra Vigne's menu ever since. It really is a winter salad, but we love it so much that we make it year round by varying the fruits and greens according to the season: Instead of cherries, we have served the salad with cherry tomatoes; grilled, sliced pears; and grilled or chopped oven-dried figs. The salad makes a festive, seasonal supper with a glass of beaujolais nouveau and crusty bread.

¼	pound pancetta, cut into ¼-inch dice
4	tablespoons porcini olive oil (page 24)
2	tablespoons chopped garlic
1	tablespoon chopped fresh thyme
⅓	cup sherry vinegar
¼	cup dried cherries
5	ounces fresh goat cheese
6	cups mixed greens, such as frisée (curly endive) and baby spinach
	Salt and freshly ground pepper

Render diced pancetta in a small sauté pan over low heat until pancetta has released its fat and the meat has lightly browned all over. Drain pancetta on paper towels and reserve 1 tablespoon of the fat in the pan.

Add 2 tablespoons of the porcini oil to the pan and heat over medium-high heat. Return pancetta to pan and cook until crispy. Add garlic and sauté until light brown. Remove pan from heat, add thyme, and stir well. Add vinegar, return pan to heat, and deglaze pan, scraping up all the brown bits that cling to the bottom and sides of the pan. Add cherries and simmer until reduced by half.

Off the heat, crumble the goat cheese into the pan and stir to break up the cheese. Add the mixed greens and the remaining 2 tablespoons porcini oil and season with salt and pepper. Quickly toss mixture well so greens barely wilt. Immediately transfer to plates and serve.

Serves 4.

MUSHROOM HASH

This is a great side dish as well as a fantastic topping for pizza or pasta, a stuffing for chicken, or a filling to layer in a lasagna.

½	cup porcini olive oil (page 24)
2	pounds fresh shiitake, domestic, or wild mushrooms, trimmed and quartered
	Salt and freshly ground pepper
2	tablespoons chopped fresh thyme or 2 teaspoons dried thyme
2	tablespoons chopped fresh flat-leaf parsley
¼	cup finely chopped garlic

Heat 2 tablespoons of the porcini oil in a large sauté pan over medium-high heat until it just begins to smoke. Add ¼ of the mushrooms; do not move them until lightly brown on one side, about 1 minute, then sauté until brown, about 5 minutes. (It is very important that the mushrooms are not crowded, otherwise they will boil in their own juices rather than brown.)

Sprinkle mushrooms with salt, pepper, and ½ tablespoon of the thyme (½ teaspoon if dried). Stir well and add parsley. Mix again and scrape into a bowl. Repeat with remaining mushrooms and oil. Add all the garlic to the last batch, sautéing until light brown. Return all the mushrooms to the pan and mix well. Season to taste with salt and pepper. Cook until heated through, if using immediately, or store, tightly covered in the refrigerator for up to 2 days.

Serves 6.

CHEF'S NOTES: *If mushrooms are dirty, do not wash them. Clean them by wiping gently with a tea towel or use an old, soft toothbrush.*

If you have a large enough sauté pan, you can cook the mushrooms in fewer batches. But you must avoid overcrowding the pan as this prevents browning and flavor development and results in soggy mushrooms.

OVEN-ROASTED
VEGETABLES

This is a wonderful, easy way to take advantage of your summer garden — almost every vegetable takes well to roasting and grilling except for delicate ones such as English peas and snap peas. Roasted winter vegetables are equally good and can make a whole supper with a piece of cheese and bread. This dish can be made several hours in advance and left, covered, on a counter to be served at room temperature. It also makes a delicious sandwich filling with Basil-Garlic Mayonnaise (page 33). Some additions or substitutions for the vegetables below include asparagus, beets, leeks, eggplant, and carrots each cut into bite-size pieces.

1	large red onion, sliced ¼-inch thick
2	small zucchini (about ½ pound total), sliced ⅜-inch thick on the diagonal
1	pound shiitake or domestic mushrooms, sliced ⅜-inch thick
1	fennel bulb, sliced ¼-inch thick, lengthwise
1	red bell pepper, seeded and cut into ½-inch julienne
¾	cup (about) porcini olive oil (page 24) Salt and freshly ground pepper
1	tablespoon finely chopped garlic
2	teaspoons fennel seed
1	teaspoon red chili pepper flakes (optional)
2	tablespoons sherry vinegar or red wine vinegar
2	tablespoons finely chopped fresh flat-leaf parsley

Preheat broiler and place rack 5 or more inches below the heat. Place onion, zucchini, mushrooms, fennel, and bell pepper in a large bowl. Pour 3 to 4 tablespoons porcini oil over and toss well to coat. Add more oil if necessary so that all vegetables have a light coating of oil. Season with salt and pepper to taste and toss again.

Spread vegetables in one layer on a baking sheet or in a roasting pan. Place in oven and roast until they begin to brown. Stir vegetables occasionally so they cook evenly and don't burn. Roast until all vegetables are cooked through, about 30 minutes. Lower rack or heat if vegetables cook too quickly.

Heat 2 tablespoons of the porcini oil in a small sauté pan over high heat until hot. Add garlic and sauté until light brown, moving the pan on and off the heat as necessary to regulate temperature. Add fennel seed and red chili pepper flakes, if desired. Let sizzle 5 to 10 seconds. Remove pan from heat and add vinegar. Whisk well, then whisk in another 5 tablespoons porcini oil, parsley, and salt and pepper to taste. Toss roasted vegetables with the dressing and serve.

Serves 6.

MUSHROOM AND ARTICHOKE PAPPARDELLE

This pasta works well as a one-dish supper. If you are looking for a more substantial dish, simply sauté some chicken or lamb pieces with the mushrooms. In the spring, I like to substitute asparagus for fresh spinach. This is a soupy pasta, terrific for dipping crusty bread.

4	large artichokes (or 4 marinated artichoke hearts if short on time)
2	tablespoons fresh lemon juice
½	cup porcini olive oil (page 24)
6	ounces fresh shiitake or domestic mushrooms, sliced ¼-inch thick (about 4 cups)
3	cups chicken stock (page 44) or canned, low-salt chicken broth
¾-1	pound dried pappardelle (wide egg pasta)
1	tablespoon finely chopped garlic
1	tablespoon chopped fresh thyme or 1 teaspoon dried thyme
	Salt and freshly ground pepper
1	bunch fresh flat-leaf parsley, finely chopped
¾	cup freshly grated Parmesan cheese
½	bunch spinach, well washed and dried

If using whole artichokes, cut off and discard the top ⅓ of the artichokes and cut off all but 1 inch of the stem. Snap off dark, outer leaves until only the pale, yellow-green leaves remain. With a paring knife, trim the artichokes and their stems of all the dark green parts. Cut in half lengthwise through the heart and remove the fuzzy chokes with a spoon. Slice the hearts lengthwise ⅛-inch thick and put in a bowl of water with the lemon juice.

In a large sauté pan, heat ¼ cup of the porcini oil over high heat until it just begins to smoke. Add mushrooms and sliced, fresh artichoke hearts, if using (marinated artichokes should be added later). Do not move them for about 1 minute or until lightly brown on one side. Then sauté until brown, about 5 minutes. (It is very important that the mushrooms are not crowded; otherwise they will boil in their own juices rather than brown.)

Meanwhile, bring chicken stock to a boil in a saucepan and boil until reduced by ½. Bring a pot of salted water to a boil for the pasta. (If you have used canned stock, *do not* salt the pasta cooking water!) Cook the pasta until al dente.

Add garlic to mushroom mixture and continue to sauté until garlic turns light brown, about 1 minute. Add thyme and reduced chicken stock. Bring to a boil and season with salt and pepper. If using marinated artichokes, add them now.

To finish, add remaining ¼ cup porcini oil, parsley, and ½ cup of the cheese. Stir well and season with salt and pepper. Stir in spinach just until it wilts and add cooked pasta. Pour onto a platter or divide among hot bowls; sprinkle remaining cheese on top. Serve pronto!

Serves 4.

PORK TENDERLOIN WITH MOLASSES, BACON, AND PORCINI VINAIGRETTE

Pork is a very sweet tasting meat and, if well trimmed, is low in fat. The agro dolci (sweet and sour) nature of the vinaigrette is a classic Italian flavor profile that works well with pork, chicken, and veal. Serve the pork with Sautéed Spinach (page 63) leaving out the bacon. Recipe may easily be doubled.

6	tablespoons porcini olive oil (page 24)
2	pounds pork tenderloin
	Salt and freshly ground pepper
½	pound bacon, cut into ¼-inch dice
1	tablespoon finely chopped garlic
1	teaspoon finely chopped fresh rosemary or ½ teaspoon dried rosemary
⅓	cup balsamic vinegar
2	tablespoons dark molasses
1	tablespoon finely chopped fresh flat-leaf parsley

Preheat oven to 400 degrees F. Heat 3 tablespoons of the porcini oil in a heavy, oven-going pan over medium-high heat until hot. Season pork with salt and pepper and brown all over, 3 to 5 minutes. Put in the oven and roast to an internal temperature of 165 degrees F, about 15 minutes.

When pork has cooked, transfer it to a platter and keep warm. Pour cooking juices from pan over meat. Return pan to medium heat and add bacon. Cook until crisp. Drain off and discard all but 2 tablespoons fat from the pan. Add garlic and sauté over medium-high heat until light brown. Add rosemary and stir. Remove pan from heat, add vinegar, and stir up all the brown bits that stick to the bottom of the pan. Add molasses and stir well.

To finish sauce, return pan to heat and stir in meat juices that have accumulated around the meat. Add parsley and remaining 3 tablespoons porcini oil. Keep warm. When ready to serve, slice meat ¼-inch thick and arrange on 4 heated plates. Spoon sauce over meat.

Serves 4.

Some lemon oils made in Tuscany are extraordinary. Whole lemons are ground along with the olives into a paste and then pressed, extracting the lemon flavor with the oil. In this process, the lemon and olive flavors become joined in a way impossible to duplicate in the home kitchen. These oils also tend to be fabulously expensive. Home-made oils emphasize the fresh, juicy character of citrus and are a particular delight for summer cooking.

All the flavors of citrus oils — orange, lemon, lime, tangerine — are essentially interchangeable. If I run out of orange, I just fill out the amount in the recipe with lemon. When using citrus oils, you are adding the flavor but not the acid. Occasionally, you may need to add back some acidity in order to balance the flavors of a dish.

Citrus oils are wonderful to dress greens with effortless panache — no vinegar necessary, just toss with a drizzling of the oil. This is particularly helpful if the dinner is an occasion when the taste of good wines may be harmed by an acidic dressing.

Citrus-flavored olive oils are distinctly different from the concentrated citrus essence oils on the market and cannot be interchanged. These concentrated oils are most appropriate for innumerable baking uses such as for flavoring cake and cookie batters, as well as frozen mousses and baked soufflés, and even for making mixed drinks with or without the addition of spirits.

ROASTED SALMON WITH GREEN BEANS AND CITRUS VINAIGRETTE

WARM NEW POTATO SALAD WITH CHIVES

MARINATED GRILLED SHRIMP COCKTAIL

ROASTED BEET SALAD WITH CITRUS-TARRAGON DRESSING

TOMATO AND RED ONION "SANDWICH"

ROASTED SALMON
WITH GREEN BEANS AND
CITRUS VINAIGRETTE

We like this salmon roasted on a hot cedar plank in the old, Native American way. The cedar gives the salmon a sweet smokiness. The preheated board allows the fish to cook evenly from the top and bottom at the same time. Following is a traditional method for roasting salmon in the oven; see Chef's Notes for instructions for roasting on a cedar plank which is also done in your home oven.

½	pound green beans, topped and tailed
7	tablespoons honey
¼	cup balsamic vinegar
½	cup citrus olive oil (page 24)
2	teaspoons lemon zest
	Salt and freshly ground pepper
4	skinless salmon fillets (5 ounces each)
2	tablespoons extra-virgin olive oil
2	handfuls mixed greens
1	teaspoon fresh lemon juice

Bring a saucepan of salted water to a boil. Add green beans and cook until tender, 3 to 5 minutes. When done, drain and spread on a baking sheet to cool.

Preheat oven to 450 degrees F. In a small bowl, combine honey and vinegar. If honey is too thick to mix easily, warm it on the stove or in the microwave oven for a few seconds. Slowly whisk in citrus oil to form an emulsion. Add zest and season with salt and pepper to taste. Pour all but 2 to 3 tablespoons into another bowl.

Season salmon on both sides with salt and pepper. Put on a dish and pour about ⅓ of the honey vinaigrette over. Turn several times to make sure salmon is well coated. Heat 1 tablespoon extra-virgin olive oil in a nonstick, oven-going pan over medium-high heat until hot. Add fillets in one layer and immediately place in oven until done, 8 to 10 minutes.

Toss green beans with a little of the remaining vinaigrette and divide among 4 plates. Place salmon on top and brush with more vinaigrette. Garnish with mixed greens moistened with remaining olive oil and lemon juice.

Serves 4.

CHEF'S NOTES: *Cedar planking salmon: Cut a 14-inch length from a 1-inch by 8-inch cedar board. To condition the board before its first use, place it on a cookie sheet and put it on the middle rack in a preheated 450 degree F oven. "Roast" the plank until it is fragrant and starts to crackle, about 8 minutes. Then remove and wipe with a cloth that has been saturated with olive oil. Place salmon on the board and return it to the oven. Cook until salmon is done, about 10 minutes. For a dramatic presentation, remove the salmon to a platter and keep warm. Let board cool a little; then arrange beans on the plank. Replace fish on top of beans, garnish with greens, and serve. Board may be washed and reused 6 to 8 times.*

Variation with Lavender Oil: This is a great recipe for lavender olive oil, which goes wonderfully with the tastes of honey, balsamic vinegar, and salmon. Replace citrus olive oil with lavender oil or use half and half.

WARM NEW POTATO SALAD WITH CHIVES

This is a terrific way to serve small new potatoes which have the sweet taste of spring. Adding the dressing to still-warm potatoes is a variation of German potato salad. The citrus oil vinaigrette is a pleasant and healthy change from a traditional American, mayonnaise-based potato salad.

1	pound small red potatoes
1	tablespoon champagne wine vinegar or white wine vinegar
¼	cup citrus olive oil (page 22)
4	shallots, thinly sliced
2	tablespoons finely chopped fresh chives
	Salt and freshly ground pepper

In a large saucepan, cover potatoes with cold, salted water and bring to a boil. Lower heat and simmer until tender when pierced with a knife, about 15 minutes.

In a small bowl, mix together vinegar, citrus oil, shallots, and chives. Season with salt and pepper to taste. When potatoes are cooked, drain and let stand until just cool enough to handle.

Slice ¼-inch thick and immediately toss with dressing. Add salt and pepper to taste and toss again.

Serves 4.

CHEF'S NOTES: *By starting the potatoes in cold water, the potatoes will cook more evenly from the inside out.*

MARINATED GRILLED SHRIMP COCKTAIL

This is the only recipe in the book that calls for cilantro (the fresh leaves of coriander), not because I don't like the herb. I do, but it is rarely used in Italian cooking. I have used cilantro in about four dishes at Tra Vigne in its seven years of existence and only used it after I found some old Sicilian recipes that called for cilantro. My guess is that people had coriander seeds from the spice trade and planted some of them.

1	pound large prawns (size 16/20 or larger), shells on
½	cup citrus olive oil (page 22)
2	tablespoons minced red onion
1	teaspoon minced garlic
2	tablespoons finely chopped fresh cilantro
2	tablespoons fresh lemon juice
4	bamboo skewers, soaked, or metal skewers
	Salt and freshly ground pepper
	Citrus Aioli (page 74), optional

Cut along the back about ¼-inch deep through the shell of each prawn to remove the vein. Put prawns in a shallow, nonaluminum baking dish.

In a small bowl, whisk together citrus oil, onion, garlic, cilantro, and lemon juice. Pour over prawns, cover, and let marinate, refrigerated, 1 to 4 hours.

Preheat grill or broiler. When ready to cook, thread prawns on skewers and discard marinade. Season with salt and pepper to taste and grill or broil, turning once, until just done, 2 to 3 minutes. Shrimp can be served warm or at room temperature. They are delicious on their own or with citrus aioli.

Serves 4 as an appetizer.

CHEF'S NOTES: *Leaving the shells on the prawns protects them from drying out during cooking. This method works so well that I use it often when preparing shrimp or prawns for salads, pasta, pizza, and sandwiches. Simply reduce the cooking time if they will later be cooked more, for instance as part of a sauce or pizza topping. Peel shrimp after they come off the grill.*

ROASTED BEET SALAD WITH CITRUS TARRAGON DRESSING

Like potatoes, beets taste best roasted in their jackets. They get incredibly sweet and peel easily once roasted. While the beets are delicious served on their own, you may arrange them on a bed of mixed salad greens or arugula to add crunch to the dish.

For a more substantial salad, crumble some goat cheese or blue cheese on top.

8	medium beets (about 2 pounds), washed and trimmed to leave on 1 inch of tops and tail
	Olive oil, for coating beets
	Salt and freshly ground pepper
2	tablespoons fresh lemon juice
2	tablespoons fresh tarragon or 2 teaspoons dried tarragon (see Chef's Notes)
½	cup citrus olive oil (page 22)
5	cups loosely packed mixed salad greens or arugula *or* 3 vine-ripened tomatoes, sliced (optional)

Preheat oven to 400 degrees F. Use your hands to coat beets in olive oil, season well with salt and pepper, and place on a baking sheet in the oven. Roast until knife tender, about 1¼ hours. Let stand until cool enough to handle. Peel beets and cut into small wedges. Place in a serving bowl or nonmetallic mixing bowl.

In a small bowl, whisk together lemon juice, tarragon, and citrus oil. Pour over beets and toss well. Season to taste with salt and pepper. Let rest at least 10 minutes to allow beets to soak up flavor. Pour off some of the dressing into another bowl and toss with greens or tomatoes. Divide greens among 4 plates and top with beets.

Serves 6.

CHEF'S NOTES: *Rehydrate dried tarragon by soaking it in the lemon juice a few minutes before mixing the dressing.*

TOMATO AND RED ONION "SANDWICH"

This dish takes advantage of the traditional Mediterranean combination of tomatoes, citrus, and onion. You can serve it again and again throughout tomato season varying it each time with different herbs, different types of tomatoes (even interlayering different colors of tomato), and choosing either lemon, orange, or tangerine citrus oil. The "sandwich" makes a charming presentation as a first course and a wonderful accompaniment to grilled chicken breasts for a light, summer supper.

1	small red onion
¼	cup fresh orange juice
	Salt and freshly ground pepper
	Grated zest of 1 orange
⅓	cup citrus olive oil (page 22)
4	large vine-ripened tomatoes (3 to 3½ inches in diameter)
¼	cup chiffonade of fresh basil (see Chef's Notes)
1	tablespoon basil olive oil (page 22), optional

Cut onion in half lengthwise, then cut each half in half crosswise. Slice lengthwise into very thin (⅛-inch) pieces. Put onion in a bowl with orange juice and salt and pepper to taste. Let marinate 5 to 10 minutes. In another small bowl, whisk together orange zest and citrus oil.

Cut a small slice off the bottoms of the tomatoes so they will stand upright. Slice tomatoes in thirds, crosswise (do not core them). Lay out slices on a board or platter and season with salt and pepper. Drizzle with zest and citrus oil and top each (excluding tomato tops) with a sprinkling of onion and basil. Reassemble tomatoes and garnish tops with basil. Drizzle each with a little basil oil, if desired.

Serves 4.

CHEF'S NOTES: *To make a chiffonade, stack several whole basil leaves on top of each other. Roll up lengthwise and cut crosswise into very thin strips.*

AL DENTE: *An Italian term meaning "to the tooth," used to describe the correct texture of well-cooked risotto and pasta. The rice or pasta should give some resistance when bitten into. When the grain or pasta is cut, there should be no trace of whiteness inside; instead it should have a consistent color.*

ARUGULA: *An herb or salad green also known as rocket and roquette. It should be gathered when young and tender and the leaves are an even medium green. It will dehydrate and go limp quickly on a store shelf if not properly stored. Only buy fresh, bright looking bunches. When young, arugula has a delicious peppery flavor, good as a salad on its own or mixed with other salad greens. When it gets older, we call it "cowboy" arugula because the pepper flavor intensifies and gets almost hot. That is the time to add it to a dish such as pasta at the last moment so the arugula just wilts.*

If you grow arugula in your garden, reseed it every three to four weeks to ensure a constant supply of young leaves. Plant it in a part of the garden that is shady: the hotter the weather, the hotter the flavor. The plants, if trimmed back, will grow new leaves but this technique also tends to increase the herb's bitterness. Watercress and baby spinach can both be substituted for arugula.

BALSAMIC VINEGAR: *A rich, full-bodied vinegar, dark in color with some natural sweetness. Originally from Modena, Italy, and very expensive because of its production* techniques and twelve-year aging, the vinegar is now mass produced and short cuts are taken to produce a similar flavor to the original. The less-expensive brands work very well in cooking; however, it is always a good idea to taste your bottle to familiarize yourself with its characteristics.

BRUSCHETTA: *Traditionally, bruschetta are slices of rustic bread grilled outdoors and drizzled with good olive oil. Topped with mozzarella, chicken livers, or mushrooms, they are often served as part of an antipasti.*

CANNELLINI BEANS: *White, oval beans, usually smallish, but I like mine large, at least ½-inch long. Bigger beans seem to have more flavor as well as having a higher flesh to skin ratio, and skins can be hard to digest. If your dried beans are old, toss them out. Old beans take much longer to cook than those from a more recent harvest. I do not consider canned beans an adequate substitute; to me, they have no texture.*

A great source for top-quality, large cannellini beans (as well as a large variety of other organic herbs, vegetables, and dried beans) is Phipps Ranch, P. O. Box 349, 2700 Pescadero Road, Pescadero, CA 94060. Call 415-879-0787 for a catalog or write. Mail order, retail, and wholesale.

CAPERS: *The flower buds of a bush native to tropical and subtropical areas. In the current fashion of cutting down on salt, it is a good idea to rinse the brine from capers and then drain. If capers are large, roughly chop them before adding to a recipe, otherwise, use them whole.*

FLAT-LEAF PARSLEY: *Also called Italian parsley. It is a variety of the common curly-leafed parsley but has dark green, flat leaves and a good, strong parsley flavor. Flat-leaf parsley is widely available in supermarkets and the curly-leafed parsley is not an adequate substitute. The parsley does grow easily in the garden from seed without bolting or going to seed too quickly. The herb can be used, when young and tender, as a vegetable on its own, as a salad with a mustard vinaigrette and freshly grated Parmesan cheese, and as a pasta topping chopped fine and added to hot pasta with roasted garlic oil. As long as there is a bunch of parsley and flavored oils in the refrigerator, it is possible to make a great meal.*

ORECCHIETTI: *"Little ears" in Italian. A circular, shallow, bowl-shaped pasta about ¼-inch in diameter. Its shape catches and holds pasta sauces; it is often served with meat sauces.*

PANCETTA: *Commonly referred to as Italian bacon. It is cured pork belly but not smoked as is American bacon. American bacon may be substituted and will add a smoky flavor to the dish. Pancetta is sold in flat pieces or rolled into rounds. Used as a flavoring for soups, sauces.*

PAPPARDELLE: *Egg noodles similar to tagliatelle and fettuccine but cut much wider, about 1 inch.*

PARMESAN CHEESE: *A hard, cow's milk cheese made in the Parma region of Emilia in central Italy. It is made only during the spring, summer, and early fall when the cows eat fresh grass. The rind forms naturally during aging. The best are aged two years before sale, but Parmesan is now being imported much younger, six to eight months old. The cheese will then have a milder taste and softer texture.*

Members of the Parmesan producers association stamp each of their cheeses on the rind with the cheese's name. To identify the real thing, look on the rind for the words (or what part you can read on the cut pieces) parmigiano-reggiano. Cheeses made outside of the small area restricted for Parmesan production and cheeses made during the winter when cows eat dry hay are called grana. These are very acceptable substitutes for Parmesan and are sometimes preferable when the dominant flavor of very aged Parmesan would detract from the effect of the entire dish. Parmesan and especially pecorino (see next page) have very high sodium contents. When a recipe calls for Parmesan, undersalt to compensate and add the cheese before the final adjustment of seasoning. When heating the cheese, do so only until it softens or turns a pale gold. If it becomes overly brown it will taste bitter. Save the rind and put it whole or cut into small pieces in soups to flavor them. The rind will soften and taste delicious.

There is not yet a domestic version of Parmesan I would use, but some good versions are made in Argentina, for instance. If you must buy grated cheese, buy that which the store has grated that day and keep it in the freezer.

PASTEURIZED LIQUID EGGS AND CHOLESTEROL-FREE LIQUID EGGS: Because of the dual threats of salmonella and cholesterol, many people have become concerned about using raw eggs and even under-cooked eggs with runny yolks such as poached or coddled eggs. The most important thing to remember is to buy fresh eggs that have been refrig-erated and to refrigerate them as soon as you get home. Use them directly from the refrigerator or leave at room temperature for no more than a few hours. The California Egg Commission (1150 North Mountain Avenue, Suite 114, Upland, CA 91786; 909-981-4923) has very good infor-mation available. Recently, pasteurized eggs have begun to be available to consumers. For many years bakeries and restaurants have been using pasteurized liquid eggs — whole eggs without the shells. The FDA requires that these products be pasteurized. While commercial establishments may buy pasteurized egg yolks, egg whites, or whole eggs, consumers, at the moment, can only purchase pasteurized whole eggs. They are packaged in cartons and sold in the refrigerated section of the supermarket. One brand in California is called Nulaid. Follow directions on the package and use the equivalent of 1 whole egg for

the mayonnaise recipes in this book. Cholesterol-free liquid eggs are readily available and work for these recipes as well. Use ¼ cup liquid egg and 1 tablespoon vinegar or lemon juice and proceed with the recipe as written. The texture is very light but the emulsion does not break and it tastes very good. There is the added benefit of enjoying mayonnaise without fear of cholesterol!

PASTINA: A tiny, pellet-shaped, dried pasta traditionally used in soups. It is sold by De Cecco as #78 Acini de Pepe.

PECORINO CHEESE: As normally sold in the United States, pecorino is an aged Italian sheep's milk cheese meant for grating. It is used for many of the same purposes as Parmesan though it has a sharper, saltier flavor. There are domestic versions of pecorino as well as imports from countries other than Italy. To find the one you like best, buy small pieces to taste and compare.

PORCINI MUSHROOMS: To an Italian, the porcini (a variety of boletus) is king of the mushroom family. They have a wonderful, aromatic, rich, gamy scent and flavor. Usually sold dried in ½-ounce or 1-ounce packages, porcini can occa-sionally be found fresh. Italians grill a whole, large porcini and serve it with garlic and herbs as a first course. Rehydrate porcini and other dried mushrooms by placing them in a bowl and pouring boiling water over them. To keep them under the surface of the water, press a paper towel down into the bowl or simply stir them occasionally. Let sit until

soft, about 15 minutes. Squeeze out water over bowl and prepare as called for in the recipe. Use the water to flavor soups, stocks, sauces, etc.

RED PEPPER FLAKES: Also called chili flakes but distinct from the chili powder blends sold in stores for making chili. I use New Mexico chili flakes. To make them at home and guarantee their heat, buy whole, dried hot chilies and grind them in a spice mill or coffee grinder reserved for grinding spices. Store in a tightly sealed jar. To toast red pepper flakes, add to hot olive oil in a sauté pan and heat just until flakes begin to move and sizzle. If not using oil, add to a hot, dry pan and immediately remove from the heat. Be sure to have your stove fan on and do not breathe the aroma — it sears your lungs! Scrape flakes onto a dish as soon as they become fragrant and slightly brown.

ROASTING RED BELL PEPPERS AND CHILI PEPPERS: Roast the peppers under a preheated broiler or over an open flame or grill, turning them occasionally until skins are charred all over. Place in a bowl, cover with a lid, and let steam to loosen the skins. When cool enough to handle, peel off the charred skins. Remove and discard core, seeds, and veins. This is most easily done standing at the sink but do not rinse peppers under water! You

will wash away half their flavor. Catch juices by working over the bowl. Tear or cut peppers into strips and put in a bowl. Pour cooking liquids over, straining out the seeds. Cover and refrigerate up to 2 days. When handling chili peppers, take care not to burn your skin. Wear gloves, do not touch sensitive parts of your face (especially your eyes), and wash hands immediately afterwards.

SHIITAKE MUSHROOMS: Asian mushrooms sold fresh and dried (sold as black forest mushrooms in Chinese markets). They have a rich, meaty flavor which makes them a welcome addition to an entrée vegetarian dish and allows them to substitute well for wild mushrooms. Shiitakes are now cultivated in the United States by a number of producers and thus are more readily available in the fresh vegetable section of well-stocked stores. Soak the dried mushrooms in warm water "to cover" (press several paper towels down on mushrooms to submerge them) 15 minutes. Squeeze mushrooms over bowl to catch the liquid, then cut off and discard stems. Slice or chop caps and cook. Strain the mushroom soaking liquid and add to your dish to give the flavor a boost.

TOMATOES, CANNED: Nothing substitutes for vine-ripened tomatoes from the garden. But in the off season when I get hungry for tomato sauce, I use canned tomatoes. It is a good idea to buy several brands of canned tomatoes and taste them to see which you like best since their sweetness and acidity will vary. In the recipes I have called for plum (Roma) tomatoes though I did some testing with the supermarket brand, S&W Red Pack. The results were excellent.

INDEX

TABLE OF EQUIVALENTS

The exact equivalents in the following tables have been rounded for convenience.

OVEN TEMPERATURES

Fahrenheit	Celsius	Gas
250	120	½
275	140	1
300	150	2
325	160	3
350	180	4
375	190	5
400	200	6
425	220	7
450	230	8
475	240	9
500	260	10

LIQUIDS

US	Metric	UK
2 tbl	30 ml	1 fl oz
¼ cup	60 ml	2 fl oz
⅓ cup	80 ml	3 fl oz
½ cup	125 ml	4 fl oz
⅔ cup	160 ml	5 fl oz
¾ cup	180 ml	6 fl oz
1 cup	250 ml	8 fl oz
1½ cups	375 ml	12 fl oz
2 cups	500 ml	16 fl oz
4 cups/1 qt	1 l	32 fl oz

US/UK

oz=ounce
lb=pound
in=inch
ft=foot
tbl=tablespoon
fl oz=fluid ounce
qt=quart

WEIGHTS

US/UK	Metric
1 oz	30 g
2 oz	60 g
3 oz	90 g
4 oz (¼ lb)	125 g
5 oz (⅓ lb)	155 g
6 oz	185 g
7 oz	220 g
8 oz (½ lb)	250 g
10 oz	315 g
12 oz (¾ lb)	375 g
14 oz	440 g
16 oz (1 lb)	500 g
1½ lb	750 g
2 lb	1 kg
3 lb	1.5 kg

LENGTH MEASURES

⅛ in	3 mm
¼ in	6 mm
½ in	12 mm
1 in	2.5 cm
2 in	5 cm
3 in	7.5 cm
4 in	10 cm
5 in	13 cm
6 in	15 cm
7 in	18 cm
8 in	20 cm
9 in	23 cm
10 in	25 cm
11 in	28 cm
12/1 ft	30 cm

METRIC

g=gram
kg=kilogram
mm=millimeter
cm=centimeter
ml=milliliter
l=liter